The Secrets of Successful Entrepreneurship

Start a Business,

Grow a Business,

Sell a Business

Other Business Books Published by The Oaklea Press

Ready, Set, Dominate: Implement Toyota's Set-Based Learning for Developing Products and Nobody Can Catch You
by Michael N. Kennedy, Kent Harmon, and Ed Minnock

Continuous Improvement Marketing
by Stephen Hawley Martin

Lean Manufacturing in Build to Order, Complex and Variable Environments
by Jorge Larco, Elena Bortolan, and Michael Studley

Leaving Your Leadership Legacy: Creating a Timeless and Enduring Culture of Clarity, Connectivity, and Consistency
by Shane A Yount

Product Development for the Lean Enterprise: Why Toyota's System is Four Times More Productive and How You Can Implement It
by Michael N. Kennedy

Lean Enterprise Leader: How to get things done without doing it all yourself
by Stephen Hawley Martin

Lean Transformation: How to Change Your Business into a Lean Enterprise
by Bruce A Henderson and Jorge L Larco

Buried Alive!: Digging Out of a Managment Dumpster
by Shane Yount, Anna Versteeg, and Debra Boggan

The Secrets of Successful Entrepreneurship

Start a Business,

Grow a Business,

Sell a Business

By

Stephen Hawley Martin

WWW.OAKLEAPRESS.COM

The Secrets of Successful Entrepreneurship: Start a Business, Grow a Business, Sell a Business © 2019 by Stephen Hawley Martin. No part of this book may be used or reproduced in any manner whatsoever without written permission except in the case of brief quotations embodied in critical articles and reviews. For information visit:

www.OakleaPress.com

Acknowledgements

I'd like to thank my 20-year-old son, Hans Stadelman Martin, for reading the manuscript of this book, pointing out typos, and for giving me suggestions to make the book more appealing to Generation Z. I'd also like to thank Paul S. Miller, former President, CEO, and the Co-founder of Dominion Youth Services, for the great suggestions he made concerning material, insights, and advice to be included.

"Profits are better than wages."
Jim Rohn [1930-2009]

About the Author

Stephen Hawley Martin can say from personal experience that entrepreneur, author and motivational speaker Jim Rohn was correct when he said, "profits are better than wages" because Stephen knows about starting, growing, and selling businesses. He was a partner and principal of The Martin Agency, creator of the GEICO Gecko, "Virginia is for Lovers," and one of the nation's top ad agencies when the Ogilvy Group purchased it for ten-times earnings. He then founded an ad agency called Hawley Martin Partners that was acquired by a New York Stock Exchange company, the Interpublic Group, following five years of rapid growth. Next, he founded The Oaklea Press Inc., a book-publishing firm he continues to operate today as editor and publisher.

In this book, Stephen explains how to use your "in-the-zone activity" to create a business. Stephen's in-the-zone activity is creating and writing, which he used in the advertising agency business and still puts to work today in book publishing. He also uses it to write books, having ghostwritten a number and authored a total of 18 under his own name. More than half a dozen of his titles have reached bestseller status in their subject categories on Amazon. He is the only three-time winner of the *Writer's Digest* Book Award, having won first prize twice for fiction and once for nonfiction. He also has won a first prize for visionary fiction from *Independent Publisher* and a first prize for nonfiction from *USA Book News*.

 Stephen wrote this book for anyone with an entrepreneurial spirit, particularly under the age of 40, that wants to do what they love while pursuing a path leading to wealth and prosperity. His goal is for you, the reader, to be able to "spend each day in your own way" as quickly as you can, with no false starts, by taking one of the paths he has set out for you with the intention of eliminating as many bumps and potholes along the way as possible.

Table of Contents

CHAPTER ONE: Your Path to Riches 11

CHAPTER TWO: Chart Your Course 22

CHAPTER THREE: Starting and Growing
a Business 35

CHAPTER FOUR: Develop the Right Attitude 56

CHAPTER FIVE: Be Conscious of
and Build Your Brand 81

CHAPTER SIX: A Short Course in
Financial Literacy 94

This Book Summarized in Brief

CHAPTER ONE 106

CHAPTER TWO 107

CHAPTER THREE 109

CHAPTER FOUR 112

CHAPTER FIVE 116

CHAPTER SIX 124

"I don't care what anyone says.
Being rich is a good thing."

Mark Cuban

CHAPTER ONE: Your Path to Riches

There's an old saying, "If you can't lick 'em, join 'em." In the context of this book that means, why complain about the richest one percent in the United States, when you can become one of them? This book will tell you how. The fact is, I believe that anyone who is capable of earning a living—of getting and holding a job—can become wealthy if he or she starts with enough time ahead and systematically takes specific actions that will be revealed in this book. To say the same thing with different words, anyone living in America can become comfortably well off by following certain steps, provided the individual does not wait too long in life to begin. This is true whether a person starts out with a mindset of scarcity or with one of abundance. The right mindset—a winner's mindset—is, however, vitally important. That's why how to achieve that mindset will be covered in an upcoming chapter. But first, it's important to understand why a big disparity in income exists between those at the very pinnacle of the income ladder and others just below them. The reason is actually quite simple. It's because the vast majority of people have a job. Think about it. Most make between $10 and $30 an hour. Even someone in a high paying job will make between $50 and $100 per hour, and that high a wage is an exception to the rule. A job that pays $100 an hour puts a person in rarified air. Consider these stats: To be in the top 10% of earners in 2019 you need to make $100,000 a year, which is about $50 per hour. To be in the top 1%, you have to make at least $250,000 annually. That's $125 an hour.

The disparity between the top 1% and the bottom 99% is that almost everyone in the 99% gets just about all their money from a job. They exchange their labor, time, and expertise for a paycheck, and let me assure you, I see nothing wrong with that. It is absolutely okay to have a job, and to stay in a job if you enjoy it and are happy with that arrangement. However, the exchange of time and labor for money is an extremely inefficient way to acquire wealth. That's why those who are rich or seek to be rich take a different approach. They don't trade their labor, time, and talent for money. They let money and others work for them. They are able to do so because we live in a free-market, capitalist country. As I write this, there are politicians who disparage this fact, but frankly, it is a major factor that has made this country the envy of the world and why so many people would like to come here to live. Fortunately for you and me and everyone already here—no matter what their background or ethnicity—because of our free-market, just about everyone has the opportunity to become wealthy. Let's hope that never changes. To get rich, a person simply has to be willing to expend the effort, and to know how to go about doing so. And that, my friend, is what I intend to explain.

In a free-market economy like ours, in order to earn more money, one must move up higher on the job ladder, and that means one must have a specialized skill. It should go without saying that the more skill, talent, and expertise someone has, the more money that person can make, provided what he or she has to offer is in demand. That is the basic law of economics: "The Law of Supply and Demand." Limited supply (not many people with the talent, skill, or expertise) coupled with high demand (something a lot of people want or need) is going to command a high price. Here are two extreme examples:

- A football quarterback that can lead an NFL team on an eighty-yard touchdown drive with less than a minute remaining on the clock, for example, can earn an annual salary in the tens of millions of dollars. Why? Because a) very few people can do that, b) people pay a lot of money to watch professional football, and c) the more a team wins, the more people will watch.
- A doctor who is accomplished at heart-transplant surgery will make perhaps thousands of dollars per hour when plying his skill. According to a Google search, a heart transplant typically costs about 1.4 million dollars. The surgeon doesn't get every penny of that, but I'm willing to bet he gets a sizable share.

It makes sense, therefore, to become highly skilled at whatever service you can provide that you have a talent or knack for and enjoy. If you haven't already determined what that is, don't worry. In Chapter Two, we will discuss how you can go about figuring out what your particular niche ought to be.

Being highly skilled is important and something to strive for, but to become wealthy—really wealthy—you need to get on something besides the job ladder. I call what you need to get on the "passive" income ladder. It's the one most rich people are on. On the passive income ladder you acquire money, and ultimately wealth, without exchanging your time, talent, and labor for it. You do this by buying or building assets that produce money for you—even while you're sleeping. This requires other people to be involved in making that money for you, and it can be accomplished in several different ways. One way is by starting and building a business.

You might, for example, build a business very slowly. Say you have identified a craft you enjoy. It could be anything from carpentry or plumbing to designing websites or creating software programs. There are hundreds of possibilities, some of which will be mentioned in an upcoming chapter. You might want to start by going to work for a company that offers the service you have identified. You should pick the company to work for not because it pays the most, but because it is the one that will give you the best opportunity to learn the business and hone your craft. There, you will be exchanging your time and labor for money while you become exceptionally good at what you do and at the same time study and learn everything there is to know about a business that requires your skill and the market it serves. You will be paid to produce work for your employer's customers, and your employer will bill those customers considerably more for your work than he will pay you for doing it. The difference is the profit your employer will keep because that's how business works.

Perhaps you think that means you are being ripped off, but the truth is you are not. There is typically a standard wage for a particular type of job that is created by the "Law of Supply and Demand." Whether you are an NFL quarterback, a heart surgeon, or a computer programmer—whatever skill you have—the demand for that skill and how many others have the same skill, will determine your wage. It's as simple as that. The employer gets the profit and you get the wage, and that's okay because the employer has made an investment in a company. He or she has taken a risk. If the business goes south, they could lose all their money. Besides that, the employer is providing you with a job while at the same time giving you the opportunity to hone your craft and learn the business. I suggest you view this as a win-win situation.

Let me say that you may find that you are happy working for someone else and do not much care about getting rich. Then keep at it. Perhaps you are risk averse and like the comfort of having a job and being able to forget about it on weekends and when you go home at night. A job gives a person a sense of identity. For many, it defines who they are. That is certainly the case with the majority of people in most developed nations. On a per capita basis, not very many people are employers. The fact is that all but a very small percentage of individuals have a job. The system works because most people like the structure and the predictability of such an arrangement. We humans tend to be creatures of habit. We leave home each weekday morning, take the same bus, train, or we drive to work. We arrive at a specified time. Everything we need to do our job is there, waiting for us. We have a job description so we know what needs to be done. We perform tasks we could probably do in our sleep. Sometimes there may be stress if, for example, a deadline is looming, but probably that doesn't happen too often. We leave at a predictable time, take the same route home, have pretty much the same dinner, watch the same TV shows, and go to bed at our regular time. Then we get up in the morning and do it all over again.

That's life for most people.

Perhaps your routine is something like that, and it's okay with you. Let me point out, however, that working for someone else may not be the safest, nor the most secure way to go. I know people, for example, who worked for large corporations for twenty years or more, made it fairly high up in the middle management ranks, and then were laid off at age 45 or 50. Why? Quarterly profits were down and the board of directors decided downsizing needed to happen, or perhaps some other issue needed to be dealt with.

It's not easy for a 50-year-old man or woman to find a new job making as much as he or she did when he or she is suddenly laid off. It's a cruel fact: Whatever your salary—let's say you make $75,000 per year—you had better be sure you are delivering quite a lot more than that in cold, hard value to the company. If not, your days very likely are numbered.

It's also important to realize that it is very difficult, if not impossible, to get rich by working for someone else—unless you are one of the top executives of a publically-traded company with stock options and a big salary. Assuming that is not the case, and isn't likely to be the case in the future, and assuming you are young enough, you can become well off—even wealthy and have a comfortable retirement—by following a simple course of action. It's one of the great things about living in America. Of course, it will likely require some sacrifice on your part—what is known as "delayed gratification." How so? Because for that to happen, you will need to live below your means and invest a significant portion of your income. What you must do before you pay your bills each month is pay yourself first. You should consider that payment as important as the one you make to pay the rent, the grocery, or the electric bill.

Always Follow a Savings & Investment Plan

Everyone, including those who plan to use a business as their wealth driver, ought to follow a savings and investment plan. If they do, they will eventually have a sizable nest egg, whether or not their business ventures are successful. That's why my advice is to put aside at least ten to fifteen percent of your income in a way that produces passive income that's continually reinvested. For example, let's say you graduate college and land a job making

$50,000 a year. That would be a typical starting salary for someone with a degree in something such as accounting, engineering, or software development. They might even make more. And let's say at age 25, you start putting away ten percent ($5000) per year in an investment fund that earns a six percent return per year on average. When you retire at age 65, you will have $825,239 in that account even though you never increased the amount from $5000 each year and have invested only a total of $200,000 (40 X $5000 =$200,000). That's the value of compounding at work. And of course, as time goes on, you are likely to get raises and eventually will make significantly more than $50,000 per year. If you continue investing ten percent of what you make each year, you will have a great deal more than a million dollars in that account when you retire.

Here's my advice: Always put the maximum amount possible into a tax-free 401(k) or other government sponsored saving plan that invests, for example, in mutual funds that are indexed to the stock market. In addition, you might allow money to build up in a savings account until you have enough to invest in rental properties. With good credit, you can put twenty percent down on a house and take out a mortgage to cover the rest. Lenders like to lend money on real estate because it gives them easily marketed collateral. Once you have a tenant, the rent he or she pays ought to be enough to cover the mortgage and upkeep, and perhaps provide an additional amount that can be invested. As time goes by, and you save more money, you can purchase more houses and rent them to people. Eventually, once the properties have been fully depreciated for tax purposes, you can cash out and invest the money in some other way. You might buy an apartment or office building or use a portion of it to take a stake in a promising startup company. An example of this way to become rich will be given in Chapter Six.

Whatever way you go, the key is to set aside money and invest it in a way that it works for you. Then keep reinvesting the proceeds, and under no circumstances withdraw any of that money until the time comes for you to retire. Barring some sort of economic collapse such as happened in 1929, and to a lesser extent in 2008, over a period of thirty or forty years you should have enough wealth accumulated to live comfortably. There will, of course, be market fluctuations, but don't panic. Just relax and ride with them. In the end, you will be fine if you do not get nervous and bounce in and out of markets or various investment options.

How to Get Rich

You can become wealthy by saving and investing, but that's the slow option, so let's assume you are not content simply with being well off and don't want to wait until age 65 before you have the ability to "spend each day in your own way." Let's say you want to be one of the fabled, "Top One Percent." Then plan to start a business. Believe me, you can do it if you want to strongly enough.

Only a tiny, one percent is at the top because most people aren't willing to do what it takes to reach such a rarified position in life. Let's face it. You will likely have to climb out on a limb to become really, really rich. But let's say you are willing to do whatever it takes, and it doesn't sit well that your employer decides how much you earn no matter how much you produce. If so, you are likely one of those courageous individuals that's willing to take risks if there is a significant chance the risks will lead to big gains. That being the case, your goal ought be to become so good at what you do that eventually you will be able to take off on your own and do what you do for customers or clients that will pay you directly for your work without an employer in the middle taking a cut. In other words, your initial goal should be to become self-employed, which is a logical Step One on the path to riches. After taking Step One, your next goal will be to grow your business to a point you cannot possibly handle it all yourself, so that it makes sense to hire someone and pay them a salary to help you service your customers. When that happens, you yourself will have become an employer.

The third goal will be to continue building the business and adding employees because being an employer with a lot of employees is what will reward you in a big way for having opted out of the employee track. Of course, this new path, the employer path, is likely to involve significant risk. It's a basic law of nature that low risk typically produces low reward and high risk can lead to high reward.

Let's use plumbing as a way to look at how this employer path might unfold. According to a quick Google search, the average "employee" plumber in a typical U.S. city earns a wage of $25 per hour, which translates to about $50,000 a year. That is not a bad salary. However, according to HomeAdvisor.com, the average charge for a plumber's services ranges between $45 and $200 per hour. The average of that is $122.50 per hour ($45 + $200 = $245 divided by 2 = $122.50). Obviously, if a plumbing company pays its employee plumbers $25 per hour and can keep them busy, quite a lot of profit will be generated for the owner.

Let's look more closely at this. Out of that $122.50 per hour, the owner of the plumbing company has to pay for expenses, such as an office, office supplies, trucks, equipment, upkeep, and repairs. The company will also likely have to have some support staff such as a bookkeeper, someone to answer the telephone and dispatch the plumbers to jobs, and someone in sales to write estimates and call on homeowners and general contractors that need plumbing work done. There may be other expenses as well. If an employer has more than 30 full-time employees, he will have to provide them all with healthcare coverage. He or she is also going to need a website, and to grow the business, advertising and promotion. On top of that, it's not likely that every hour of a plumber's forty-hour week is going to be billable because there's going to be travel time and down time between jobs, and things may be slow at certain times of year. So let's say that only three quarters (75%) of a plumber's time is going to get billed. If that is the case, the cost of a plumber to his employer will actually be $31.25 for each hour billed ($25 + 25% of $25 or $6.25 = $31.25). This leaves $91.25 per hour billed ($122.50 − $31.25 = $91.25) to cover the cost of the office, trucks, equipment, upkeep, repairs, support staff, advertising and promotion, social security, and perhaps healthcare coverage as well as other expenses. We'll call these ancillary costs "overhead."

Let's say that overhead accounts for a third of the $122.50 per hour billed or $40.83, meaning the employer is making $50.42 on every hour billed ($122.50 − $40.83 − $31.25 = $50.42). Therefore, if three-quarters of a plumber's time is billed, the employer is making $1512.60 per week on a plumber. (40 hours x 75% = 30 and 30 hours x $50.42 = $1512.60.) Multiply that by 52 weeks, and that's $78,655.20 per plumber per year. So a company with ten plumbers is making almost $800,000 (10 x 78,655.20 = 786,552) in profit per year based on this scenario. The owner ought to be able to get by quite comfortably on that and reinvest a good deal of it in assets that produce even more income. This is the compounding effect of success—money on money on money—success on success on success.

Some people may see this arrangement and this much profit as unethical, but it is not. In the first place, nothing is stopping the plumbing company's employees from becoming self-employed, or from going into business for themselves. The employer has risked his money to create a business. He or she is providing jobs for plumbers and the support staff. He his not forcing anyone to work for him, they are doing so voluntarily. He's giving them the tools they need to do their work and bringing them plumbing jobs to work on. No doubt he is paying them a fair market wage based on the going rate for plumbers in whatever area of the country they happen to live. If not, nothing is stopping them from going to work for someone else. Moreover, no one knows when a recession might hit, causing real estate developers to cut back or stop building new houses, and not need plumbing work. A recession would likely cause homeowners to postpone having updated bathrooms installed or having major plumbing projects done. To save money in troubled times, they might elect to do routine plumbing jobs themselves. These sorts of things happen in normal market adjustments. Depending on the severity, it could lead to the plumbing company owner suddenly finding himself in a downward spiral that could land him in bankruptcy.

But entrepreneurs don't spent time and energy worrying about bad things that might happen, and if growing a business is the path you decide to follow, you are an entrepreneur. Entrepreneurs think positive thoughts and consider the possibilities. So put negative thoughts out of your mind and spend your time and effort getting very, very good at your particular craft or skill because that's the best defense against market fluctuations.

Now let's begin to map out your path to riches because that's what the next chapter is about.

CHAPTER TWO: Chart Your Course

Now you know why most people will never get rich. It's because they have a job. Most people in the Top One Percent don't have jobs—they don't work for money; they let money work for them. People in the bottom 99 percent typically live in families in which the primary breadwinner works for a living. If that was true for you growing up, chances are one or both of your parents had a job, and because they considered that to be normal—the way life works—they probably encouraged you to work hard, to get a good education, and to get as high-paying a job as possible. Seems like the American way, doesn't it? And in fact it is a smart starting option—a good way to start out in life.

"Work hard and get a good education" is sound advice, but I suggest that it should not be the end game—not, that is, if you want to be truly wealthy and free to spend each day in your own way. Your education and work experience ought lay the foundation for a bigger future—one in which you have your own business.

It is a fact that most people are not particularly happy in their jobs. Instead, they are trudging through life, putting one foot in front of the other, dreading the approach of Monday mornings. According to a 2017 survey, the vast majority of the 17,000 U.S. workers in 19 industries who participated in a study conducted by the nonprofit group Mental Health America and the Faas Foundation said they are unhappy with their jobs. They are so unhappy that 71 percent said that they are looking to change employers. And that's a lot better than workers worldwide. According to a 2017 Gallup poll, 85 percent are "emotionally disconnected from their workplaces." In other words, 85 percent of workers worldwide are pretty much going through the motions at their jobs.

Don't let that happen to you. If you are in a job you hate, it's time to change. If you are just starting out, don't simply chase the money. If you love teaching, for example, do not become an accountant just because it pays more. Do what you love, but realize that as long as you are working for someone else, whether it's "The Man" or the government, you may enjoy what you are doing—which means you are better off than 85 percent of workers in the world—but you are not likely to get rich unless you incorporate other activities as part of your plan, such as investing in real estate, or you have a business on the side. We will, by the way, discuss both these possibilities in upcoming chapters.

Okay, so what if you want to do what you love and also become wealthy? Then you need to figure out what you enjoy doing and then find a way to spend your time doing it that will make you rich.

As mentioned, most people get up on Monday mornings, go to work the same way, do what the boss tells them to do, they come home, eat dinner, watch television, and go to bed burned out. The next morning, they do it all again. Keep that up and before you know it, thirty or forty years will have passed. The way to prevent that catastrophe is to call a "timeout," and take time to stop and think. When I say this, I am not talking about your morning or afternoon meditation time, or the time you spend on the bus, or on the train, or in your car driving to work. I'm talking about serious time. I'm talking about taking an entire day.

Take Time to Plan Your Life

As soon as possible, once you have finished reading this book, set aside a full day. It might be a Saturday or a Sunday, or some other day you have off from work. Plan to spend six to eight consecutive hours alone. Go to a library or some other secluded place. Leave your cell phone and computer in the car because you don't want to be disturbed. Take a pen and a legal pad, find a quiet spot, and get comfortable. You are there to decide what to do with the rest of your life.

Nothing is more important.

Here are some sample questions you might ask and answer. Spend some serious time with any you decide to tackle:

- Where is my life headed right now?
- Do I have a purpose? If so, what is it? Am I doing what needs to be done to accomplish it?
- If I had one month to live, what regrets would I have?
- Am I happy, and if not, why not?
- Am I getting out of life all life has to offer?
- Do I love my job and love getting up on Monday mornings? If not, why not? What can be done about it?
- What are my goals, desires and passions?
- If money were not an issue, what would I really want to do with my life?

A man I know was prompted to take action and pursue a new path after he considered what it would be like if he remained on the path he was on, lived out his life, and then looked back at it from his death bed at age 98.

He asked himself, "What regrets would I have?"

"Plenty," he realized. And so he went to work to chart a totally new course.

Let's say you have done some similar soul searching and you also decide that you need to change course. If so, the time has come to ask the big question, the answer to which should help you create the best possible plan for your life going forward:

What have I done that puts me so totally in the zone that when I finish, I look up and see that hours that have passed and it seemed like only minutes?

It may take a while for you to put your finger on that activity—the one you become totally engulfed in and absorbed by—but once you do, you are halfway to figuring out what to do to get rich. When you ask that question, think back over your life. If necessary, go all the way back to when you were a child. Write down everything you enjoyed doing, and I mean everything that comes to mind. Do not self-edit; take your time.

Taking time and having time to take is important because your mind works differently when you feel rushed because of a looming deadline. It's virtually impossible to go deep with a clock ticking in your head. This is also something you cannot do riding in a car to and from work or the grocery store. As stated above, you need to be in a quiet place—maybe a study room or a cubical in a library—someplace you will not be disturbed.

Before you address this question, sit back and relax. Take a deep breath and hold it to the count of four. Then let it out slowly through your mouth. Your frame of mind needs to be that there's nothing else to do or to think about. It's important to step outside yourself—figuratively speaking—and to take an objective look at your life up until now so that you can pinpoint past activities that put you in the zone. Let your point of view float out of the top of your head, rise high above it, and take a long, objective look at your life, starting as far back as you can remember.

Then ask the question above and start writing what pops into your head. Once you reach a point when you cannot think of anything else, go back, look over what you have written and arrange the items in descending order with the one that stands out the most at the top of the list. Once you have identified what that is, what you will need to do is figure out how to use that activity in service to others.

That's how it will make you rich.

It seems to me just about everyone has a talent or gift they were born with that puts them in the zone. It is what we each have to give or to share with others. People who use their gift in such a way may become rich and famous, but nevertheless, they are likely to feel the acclaim is not really deserved because they so thoroughly enjoy what they do, and it comes so naturally to them. It's something they would do even if they didn't get paid for it, assuming they didn't need money to live. People who are using their gift are passionate about what they do, as though it were a flame burning in them. They lose track of time. They're in the flow.

There you have it. Identify your gift and develop a plan to get off the job track and onto the path of creating a business that not only puts your in-the-zone activity to work, but also allows you to recruit others to help accomplish your mission. Pursuing a passion—something you are truly enthusiastic about—will create a sense of purpose that will act like a magnet to attract others who will want to join in the effort. I have seen it happen. A group pulling together like a championship team to achieve a particular goal can accomplish amazing things.

As you think about what that business might be, it may be helpful to realize that there are basically only four types of businesses. They were identified and described by Litt Thompson in his book, *GET OFF THE FREEWAY: Take the Five Hour Challenge that Will Change Your Life Forever.* Have a look. Only two kinds are worth serious consideration as the types of business you may wish to start:

Category 1: High-Energy, Low-Margin

A High-Energy, Low-Margin business is one that is complicated, employee intensive, capital intensive, inventory intensive, very competitive, and to make things even worse, it doesn't make much money. Being stuck in a high-energy, low-margin business might be compared to being chained to a job you hate so don't start or go into a business that falls into this category. It's like being held captive, with a great deal of stress, and very little or no profit to show for it.

Many types of retail stores and chains fall into this category. The most vivid example is a grocery chain located in a market that has a lot of competitors, including Wal-Mart and other discount stores. The sheer size of big box stores makes it work for them, and so it makes no sense to try to compete. An enormous amount of money has to be tied up in inventory in order to have all the things people may want to buy, and almost everyone that shops in a grocery store is looking for the lowest price possible. After all, Tide Laundry Detergent is Tide Laundry Detergent—why would you pay more than you have to? According to a Google search, the average profit margin on grocery items is only one to two percent.

Manufacturing falls into this category as well. As you may know, many companies that sell manufactured goods do not do their own manufacturing. They design their products, and then contract out the manufacturing of them either domestically or to firms overseas. The result is that the competition is fierce and the margins are low.

Category 2: High-Energy, High-Margin

The High-Energy, High-Margin category is one that is complicated and employee intensive. Some businesses in this category also require a significant investment of capital, but nevertheless, high-energy, high-margin businesses can make a lot of money. Included are real estate development and construction; the building trades—plumbing, electrical, mechanical, HVAC, etc.—road building; and perhaps if done on a large scale, body and fender and auto (mechanical) repair. The more employees that can be kept busy, the more money that will be made because a profit is made on each one. A downside, of course, is that keeping tabs on a lot of employees—some of whom may not be all that reliable—can be like herding cats. That's what can make these businesses tricky.

A few additional business types that likely fall into this category are: Information Technology, Nursing, Graphic Design, Advertising, Janitorial Services, Tech Support, Website Development, Market Research, Search Engine Optimization (SEO), and Landscaping Services.

Category 3: Low-Energy, High-Margin

The Low-Energy, High-Margin category is the best one to be in if you can pull it off. Creativity and brainpower drive these businesses, and they are easily scalable. Typically, tech companies, software companies, and some import-export companies fit into this category. Apple Computer is a prime example. High tech tools of all kinds that are developed and designed in the U.S., manufactured in low-wage countries around the world such as China and Vietnam, and sold through retailers across the USA can be gold mines. So are companies that rely on specialty software such as Uber/Lyft, Google, Facebook, Bird Scooters, HubSpot, and Airbnb. Videographers that publish on YouTube can make a lot of money from advertising if they develop audiences that are large enough, and they can grow a business by also making videos for others. Bloggers that build a large audience can make good money with advertising, too, but the problem is that blogging is a business that is not easily scalable. It's typically a one man or woman band so it can only grow so large.

Real estate can be a Low-Energy, High-Margin business if you have some money to invest. For example, you might save enough to put a down payment on a house that you can rent. Make sure that the rent you will receive will be enough to pay the mortgage, upkeep, and yield at least a small profit. After a while, you can buy another rental house, and another. Then, when the mortgages are paid down, you can sell the houses and use the proceeds as a down payment on an office or an apartment building that will deliver serious income that you can invest in even more real estate. More will be said about this in Chapter Six.

Book publishing also can fall into the Low-Energy, High-Margin category. Now that Amazon will print publishers' books from PDF files when they are ordered and will convert Microsoft Word documents into Kindle eBooks to be downloaded, no capital outlay is required to start a book publishing business. All that's needed is content that people want and are willing to buy, and of course, smart promotional activities that break through the tremendous amount of clutter and noise created by the many books being offered for sale nowadays.

Category 4: Low-Energy, Low-Margin

A Low-Energy, Low-Margin business is one that's fun and easy, but doesn't make much money. An example would be a travel agency. Back when travel agencies were still around, they didn't require a lot of work because the airlines did most of it for the owner. It was also a fun business because you got to travel a lot and were wined and dined while writing off almost everything. But it was an incredibly low margin business and today most have gone under because the Internet changed everything.

Another business that might be fun for some people is a bakery, but according to *Forbes* magazine, the typical bakery makes only a 2.3 percent margin. Someone I know opened a cupcake shop in a busy pedestrian area of a city. It seemed to be a great location, but she had to close her shop after one year. It's tough to be successful in a business that has a built-in low margin when no matter how much time and energy the owner invests only moves the dial a little.

Let's say you have determined your gift and how you can put it to work in service to others in Category 2, or better yet, in a Category 3 business. What will it take for you to get off the job track, and onto the path to owning a business of your own? It will take time, and it will take a plan. So identify the obstacles and work out a step-by-step plan and timetable to get around them.

This may not be something you will have time to do in your first library session. So keep taking full-day sessions as often as possible in order to get a detailed plan down on paper. Then, once you have one written, I suggest you set aside a full day once each month to update, add to, and refine it.

Obstacles Point to Your Path

Obstacles are what you want to pinpoint as you go about this exercise. Once you identify them, the hard work is done because now all you need to do is figure out ways to get around them, over them, or under them. The course you devise to skirt the obstacles standing between you and your goals will be your action plan—the path to take to get where you want to go.

Let's say you want to be a substance abuse counselor and the obstacle is that you don't have the right degree. You need to figure out a way to get that degree—that's your path. A middle-aged guy I know who spent the first part of his life as a radio disc jockey was able to do just that. Now he is self-employed and has a contract with the prison system to counsel inmates in the state where he lives. As his reputation and contacts grow, his plan is to hire counselors and put them to work like the plumber in Chapter One.

Perhaps, you say, getting a specialized degree or a certification of some kind is what you need, but you don't have the money.

You have just identified the obstacle: money.

A mechanical engineer that worked at General Motors designing cars decided in his thirties that he wanted to be a doctor. He sold his house so he could use the equity from it, and he also took out college loans. It was a long grind and wasn't easy, but he is now a doctor, happy as can be, making a ton of money, and starting to bring in more physicians in order to grow his practice.

Maybe you have identified a type of business in which you could use your gift but you have never worked in the field and do not know much about the business of the business. Take a job in the field, not for the money, but to learn. Work to hone your craft while you learn the industry, make contacts and build a solid reputation. Your goal should be to become an expert, the go-to person in that line of work.

Another option is to partner with an expert. Find a way to align yourself with someone who has the credentials, contacts, and network you lack. Build a team of people who each bring something unique and valuable to the enterprise, and you soon will have a business. You don't have to have all the skills yourself. You just have to have someone on your team who has the ones you don't.

Here's another idea. Let's say you are working to learn. Perhaps the owner of the business is getting up there in age and would like to sell the firm if he only had a buyer. If you bring up the idea, he or she might see you as a possible exit ramp. You might be able to work out a deal to buy the business over time. If not, at some point you will want to leave and become self-employed with the objective of building your clientele and eventually hiring other workers.

The truth is that at some point all businesses are for sale. Often a business owner feels trapped. He or she likely has a lot of balls in the air and is tired of the stress and strain. They'd like to unload the business but don't want to put it on the market through a broker because his or her employees would find out and might start looking elsewhere for jobs. The fact is the best businesses to buy are probably not listed for sale for that reason.

That's why if a particular business interests you, it may make sense to call on and talk to the owner. Tell them you are interested in the industry and would like to learn more about it. Ask if you can pick their brain. Take the owner to lunch and talk. You might tell him or her you'd like to own a business like the one they have someday and wonder if they have ever thought about selling. You may be surprised to learn the owner is interested. He or she might even be willing to bring you on as a sort of apprentice or understudy with the intention of turning the business over to you at some point in the future. You could help grow the business while the owner eases out of it, and then buy the business over time with the profits. It would not be the first time something like that has happened.

In summary, it's very likely you have a talent, something you are especially good at, something you can do better than anyone else. At a deep level, you know what it is because it's buried in your subconscious mind. Putting it to work in service to others can be your purpose in life as well as your path to wealth. All you have to do is figure out what it is and the best way to use it to help others, and to get others to help you. There is no rule in life that you have to do everything by yourself. The better you are at bringing in others, the more you can capitalize on everyone else's talents. That has certainly been the case in advertising agencies I've been a partner in and owned. Ultimately, what you want is to create a team that cannot be beaten.

You can begin by taking the time to think deeply and to develop a plan. Understand and accept that this will take time and it will take perseverance. Set aside a day-a-month for library time. Review your life. Think about the decisions that brought you where you are today and where the new decision you have made, and the goals you have identified, are going to take you.

As you reach each goal, keep fleshing out and updating your plan. Post your goals for the week or the month on your bathroom mirror where you will see them each morning. Keep at it, and it will happen. Persistence and focus will get you there.

In the next chapter we will consider the best way to start a business. We will look at a few examples of what others have done and see what can be learned from them so that you will be in position to start and grow your business into a powerhouse.

CHAPTER THREE: Starting and Growing a Business

Some people do not take the time to figure out what activity puts them in the zone, and they don't spend the time and effort to systematically plot a course for starting and growing a business. Maybe that's why half of all new businesses fail within the first five years, according to the Small Business Association (SBA). But that is a lot less likely to happen to you if you take the time to think things through and get your ducks in a row. Your goal ought to be to start a business that will begin making money immediately with enough potential customers who want what you have to sell for it to grow and expand, right from the start.

Of course, it's likely you will have to start small and grow your clientele. To do so you need to offer customers true value in order to generate positive word of mouth and keep them coming back. And your business needs to be scalable—in other words, it ought to be organized in such a way that it can easily expand. You also ought to have in the back of your mind that someday you are going to sell the business and cash out so that you will be able to "spend each day in your own way." In other words, it's important to have an exit strategy and to incorporate it into your plan. You might set some sort of target to aim for so that when you reach it you will know the time has come, and you have achieved your goal. In this chapter we will look at how others have done this.

First, let's consider a man I'll call Ralph and what he was able to accomplish. He was an average kid who did all right in school—nothing spectacular—but he got into college, and with Pell Grants, student loans, and a part time job, he was able to pay tuition, room, and board. He had no idea what he wanted to do in life, but there was one thing he was sure about. He didn't want to take biology and other sciences if he could help it. They were just not his thing. He soon found that he could avoid having to take those courses if he enrolled in the business school of his university, and so that is what he did. He hadn't given any thought to his passions or in-the-zone activities, but he did find that he liked the business courses he was taking, in particular those that had to do with finance. Money and finance, it turned out, was a field he could get caught up in, and because he liked it, he excelled at it. He actually started making top grades for the first time in his life. As a result, he decided to make finance his major.

An Industry Where Ralph Put His Passion to Work

After graduation, Ralph took a job at a bank. After completing an in-house management-training course, it wasn't long before he became a loan officer, and the unit he was assigned to made loans primarily to construction firms—companies that built houses, apartment buildings, office parks, and such. To get a loan, these companies would put together a prospectus for Ralph to review that laid out in detail their projected costs, what they expected a house or building to sell for based on comparable sales taking place in the market, and the return in the form of profit they could expect to make upon completion and the sale of a building.

Needless to say, Ralph soon learned the ins and outs of building construction finance. He also saw how much money there was to be made, and being someone who liked and understood finance, Ralph decided he ought to go into the construction business himself. So, as suggested in the previous chapter, he spent a few Saturdays and bank holidays in the library to plot his course.

As Ralph sat in a cubical in the library on one of those days listing his assets, he realized he was a whiz at finance, he understood the financial ins and outs of building and construction, and that he knew what things cost and how much time was required for certain phases of construction. He even understood from an insider's point of view what banks were looking for and the requirements banks had when it came to making construction loans. He also realized there was something very important he was missing. Ralph had saved some money, and he already had a building project in mind that he thought would get the construction company he had in mind off to a good start. The problem was—the obstacle—was that he knew very little about the nuts and bolts—the nitty-gritty—of construction. He had the big picture down pat, but how did you actually take an architect's drawings and turn them into a finished building? He also realized he did not have contacts in the building trades that would be needed, such as the plumbing contractors, electrical, and HVAC companies. His lack of knowledge and contacts was the obstacle standing in his way.

How could he get around it?

Ralph Finds a Way to Overcome the Obstacle

It dawned on Ralph that he knew someone in high school, a classmate of his I'll call George, who had gone to Virginia Tech to study Building Construction. With a little detective work, Ralph learned that George was now working for a big construction firm, apparently doing quite well. George was creating a solid reputation for himself as someone who knew his stuff. Ralph realized George could be the path around the obstacle.

Ralph put together a plan that laid out all the numbers, including the profit they could potentially make by working together, and he invited George to go to lunch. To make a long story short, they agreed to go into business, and over the course of 25 years, they built a real estate development and construction firm that eventually had offices in two states and built hundreds of houses a year as well as apartment and office buildings. They sold that firm for more than $200 million. Ralph put his share in investments that produce an enormous amount of passive income. Now both Ralph and George spend each day in their own ways.

    Ralph did several things you might want to keep in mind, and perhaps emulate, as you develop a plan to start and then to grow your business. He began with something he was good at doing and enjoyed—finance—and used it to become an expert—a go-to guy—concerning the financial aspects of construction. Then he found someone to partner with, George, who was an expert in the fundamentals and details of construction, which Ralph didn't know in depth. Supervising and directing construction workers and sub contractors in order to bring an architect's drawings to reality was George's expertise and something that put him in the zone. And so you might say Ralph and George's partnership was a perfect match.

    This brings up a cardinal rule—perhaps THE cardinal rule—to keep in mind as an entrepreneur: When it comes to selecting a partner or a key employee, always choose someone who knows more about the job they will be doing than you do. This is a rule my brother David and I followed at the advertising agencies we started and ran, and I can say with absolute certainty it was the fundamental reason for the success of those businesses. We brought on future industry giants like Harry Jacobs, Mike Hughes, Don Just, John Adams, and many others who went on to become top performers in the field of advertising.

If you take only one piece of advice from this book, I urge you to do this: make it a point to surround yourself with people who are smarter than you if at all possible, and at the very least, make sure they are the best people in their fields that you can find and attract. And don't be a micro manager. If you want to grow a business, you cannot do everything yourself. You have to be willing to turn things over to others and let go. Hire smart people, and promote smart people. Give them all jobs to do—areas of the business for them to manage—and make it worth it to each one by providing them with incentives to do a top job. You do not want to become an owner who is trapped by his or her business. What you want is to build a business that runs itself. The ideal business to own, as I see it, is one that you could leave for six months, and when you come back, it would be better than when you left. Think how much easier it will be to sell a business like that and how much more money you will likely get for it.

Here's something else to remember: Whatever you measure and focus on will expand, and so you might offer bonuses to managers based on achieving specific goals. Do not give up equity in your business if you can help it. Instead, you might give a key person a share of the profits so that he or she will become highly motivated. Then, once employees have the tools they need and incentives to perform, by all means get out of the way—turn them loose. If they have what it takes, you won't go wrong with this approach.

This is s fundamental principle to put work that I call "leverage"—people-leverage and money-leverage. Smart businesspeople leverage the brainpower, expertise, and the drive to succeed of others. Another kind of leverage—money leverage—has to do with putting to work and using other people's money to grow your business. You will recall, for example, that in addition to leveraging George's building construction expertise, Ralph benefited from leveraging money. By understanding what was important to banks when it came to lending money for construction, he as able to develop construction-financing proposals that bank loan officers viewed as solid, and in that way he was able to put other people's money to work to build his business.

Staffing Businesses

There are a number of businesses you might consider going into, depending on your particular area of expertise, that look a lot like the plumbing business described in Chapter One. The person who started it first worked for a plumbing company in order to learn the business. Then he left and went on his own, becoming self employed, and he built up his clientele to the point he needed to hire other plumbers to help him get all the work done. Next, he went to work drumming up even more business through sales calls, advertising and promotion, and as the business grew, he hired more plumbers and sent them to work on jobs where they were needed. He was able to charge enough based on market rates to cover a an employee plumber's wage, the cost of support staff and overhead, including advertising and promotion, to a make pretty good profit. The more plumbers he could keep busy, the more money he made. With ten plumbers, he was pulling in almost $800,000 a year.

There are plenty of other fields in which it may be possible to do something similar. An advertising agency is based on the same model. In a way, such companies might be thought of as, "Staffing Businesses." You hire staff with specific skills—like plumbing or copywriting—and "rent" them out to businesses or individuals that need work done that require those skills.

If you decide to go this route, an important key is to find an industry that provides a service that's in demand. You should really know your way about the particular industry you select, or at the very least partner with someone who does. Then you need to drum up business, hire staff, promote, drum up more business, and place your staff where they are needed. I cannot over emphasize how important it is to hire good people, especially supervisors, give them the tools they need, an incentive to perform, and then turn them loose. The more workers you can keep busy, the more money you will make. Also, if you ever intend to sell the business, you don't want it to be dependent on your running it. As previously mentioned, it is better to build a business that runs itself, which will be much more attractive to potential buyers.

Homeowners and building contractors definitely need plumbers, which is why that business worked so well. Other fields that come to mind in no particular order include Information Technology, Nursing, Graphic Design, Janitorial Services, Website Development, Market Research, Search Engine Optimization (SEO), Landscaping Services, Electrical Contracting, Tech Support, Video Production, and of course, Advertising.

No doubt there are many others.

The Young Man Who Wanted to Work for Himself

Jason was a lot like Ralph. He was not a great student, he didn't know what his passion or in-the-zone activity was, and he had no particular cause or mission he wanted to pursue. But, for some reason, he did know he did not want to work for someone else, and that he had a burning desire to accumulate wealth. So he went into the business school at his university with the idea that as soon as possible after graduation he would own a business.

Jason earned money to cover many of his college expenses as a desk clerk and bell hop at a hotel where he got to know the owner, who also happened to own two other hotels in and around the city where Jason went to school. The one where Jason worked and the other hotels had vending machines in corridors and alcoves where guests could buy chips, cookies, candy, and other snacks at any time of the day or night. The owner liked Jason, trusted him, and gave him the job of servicing the vending machines at all three of his properties, which of course meant Jason had to handle a good deal of cash. The job involved loading the machines and emptying out the money. As a result, he learned the vending machine business.

When spring came during Jason's senior year, and with graduation approaching, he began looking for some sort of business to buy. This was before the Internet, and so he searched the "Business Opportunities" listings in the classified advertising section of his local newspaper. One day he came across a vending machine route for sale. After negotiating with the owner, he was able to buy thirty machines and the truck to go with them for very little money down.

As a brand new college grad, Jason spent each day driving around, loading candy machines, drink machines, and cigarette machines. It took about twenty hours a week to fill them, but that wasn't all that was involved. He was a one-man band who not only had to load the machines, he had to fix them when they broke, and often he had difficulty with that.

When Jason got home, he had to count the money, put the coins in coin wrappers, and there were other tasks. He had to go to the bank, keep the books, order merchandise, take deliveries, load the truck, and on and on. He wanted to grow the business, but he didn't have time to make a lot of sales calls, and when he did land a new account, he'd have to install a machine, a task that was almost impossible for one person to do by himself. So he'd call on a friend to help him put one in place. It was hard, time-consuming work, and he realized very quickly he needed to build a bigger business so that he could hire someone to help.

In the little spare time he had, he looked for another vending business to buy and found one after about nine months. Jason didn't have a lot of money, but a motivated seller was selling the business and so they were able to work out a payment schedule. This enabled Jason to put his existing route together with the new one, which came with an employee who knew a lot about vending machines and turned out to be a tremendous help and pretty good at sales. One thing led to another, and before long Jason bought two more vending businesses the same, low-down-payment way. Eventually, he had a sizable business going with a number of employees working for him.

Jason says that now, in retrospect, he realizes that he actually doesn't like running businesses. What he really likes—his in-the-zone activity—is finding and negotiating deals, and so he continued looking for business opportunities. One day he noticed a telephone answering service for sale in the "Business Opportunities" section of the newspaper.

He thought, "Telephones. Technology. Electronics. I like electronics. Why not?"

The business was losing money, but he bought it anyway. This, by the way, confirmed something that has been touched on. When someone is looking for a way to exit a business, they are usually willing to cut a deal.

Before long, Jason came across another telephone answering service that was losing money. He bought it, put the two together to cut overhead, and diversified into voicemail, which was brand new at that time, paging, and cell phones, which where just coming out. They each cost $2,000 dollars apiece and were huge in size, and the working parts were so big they had to be mounted in the trunk of an owner's car.

It wasn't long before the company was no longer just an answering service, it was full-fledged telecommunications company building momentum. Jason was spending less time with the vending company—his first employee essentially was running it—and so he continued looking for telecom companies to buy with as little money down as possible.

The telecommunications business was hot back then, but it was also stressful and difficult. It was employee intensive and operated twenty-four hours a day, seven days a week. Jason would get a call at three o'clock in the morning telling him the computer system was down, which meant the phones were not working for the entire client base of doctors, lawyers, and business owners. He would jump out of bed and go to the office as fast as he could to try to reboot the system. It was extremely stressful, but he was too busy running the business to see how demanding it was.

Five or six years went by, and Jason was approached by the representative of a company located in a city a hundred and fifty miles away that wanted to buy the business. Jason was not looking to sell, but the offer was so generous that he decided to do so, anyway.

Until then, Jason had never thought about selling a business because he hadn't bought businesses to sell them, he'd bought them to run them and make money. But he learned something important because of that transaction. Being on the selling end of a sale is euphoric. He had built something up, gone through all that difficulty and stress, and sold it. Jason recalls stopping for lunch on the way back from the city where the deal was closed. Sitting in a booth with the check in his hand, a sense of total euphoria flooded over him. Like one of Pavlov's dogs, the dopamine-inducing experience of completing the full cycle of buying, building and selling a business became firmly cemented in his psyche. He says that when you buy one, you release a lot of cash and you take on stress, worry, and anxiety. It's a double whammy. But when you sell, you release all the stress and receive a lot of cash. It's a double plus. You get a big pile of money and you are no longer the captive of a business. A huge weight is lifted—the worry and the anxiety are gone! Naturally, Jason went looking right away for other businesses to start or buy, build, and then sell.

A word of caution comes with this tale. Jason built up a number of businesses, sold them, and he became very, very rich. He is now worth hundreds of millions of dollars—maybe even more than hundreds of millions. But at one point he almost lost it all. He owned four businesses at the time and all of them were cross-leveraged. In other words, he owed a bank a lot of money and all four of the businesses he owned at the time were the collateral, That's when a recession hit. Before long, sales went down—way down. Two of the businesses were losing a lot of money, and he was having difficultly making the loan payments. It got so bad his lawyer advised him to declare Chapter Eleven bankruptcy, which Jason definitely did not want to do. Fortunately, he was able to work something out with the bank and eventually the businesses recovered without Jason having to go bankrupt. But he almost had a nervous breakdown during that time, and he says that if he had to do it over again, he would do some things differently. First, he would not have gone so far out on a limb by borrowing so much money, and second, he would have been more careful about the types of businesses he bought. The two big money losers during the recession were in the "High-Energy, Low Margin" category discussed in Chapter Two. Jason says he will never again invest in a business in that category. Now he looks for, and either buys or starts businesses only in the "Low-Energy, High-Margin" category.

Selling a Business

Before I tell you one more story about a business startup, let me share with you some words about selling a business. I realize you may think you want to keep your business and pass it on to your children and future generations, but think about this. Often a business a mom or dad created will not be one that puts his or her children in the zone. As the old saying goes, "Different strokes for different folks." When that's the case, if the second generation doesn't run the business into the ground, the third generation often will. That's why it can make a lot of sense to quit while you're ahead and sell the business. In other words, cash out and put the money into passive income investments.

So let's say the time has come to sell. There are plenty of companies out there that will help you sell your business, and so before you select one, you would be wise to talk to a number of them, let them give you a sales pitch, and contact their references. Since they all take a percentage of the sale in the same way real estate agents do when they sell houses, it's in their interest to put together a proposal for you to review that explains how they intend to get as much for your business as possible. Hiring the right team and the right company is important. That's why it's also important to know what type of company will make the most sense when it comes to selling yours. There are basically three kinds that might help you sell: business brokers, M&A advisors, and investment bankers.

Business brokers typically work with smaller companies, businesses that will likely be purchased by an individual buyer, rather than a corporation. Restaurants, retail shops, convenience stores, and gas stations are examples that fall into this category. The process that business brokers use is very similar to that of listing a house for sale, and the terms are similar. Typically, business brokers sell companies that are meant to produce income for an owner/operator, and the selling price is usually based on how much cash flow will come to the owner/operator once he or she is in charge and running the operation. Information is collected about the business to be sold and the company is advertised for sale on websites and marketed with an asking price.

Typically, business brokers handle sales that are $2 million or less, investment bankers handle those above $250 million, and M&A advisors work in the gap between the two. Investment bankers will likely offer a broader range of services than M&A advisors since they work with larger companies.

M&A advisors and investment bankers typically buy and sell companies to and for other companies or institutional investors such as private equity funds. Both M&A advisors and investment bankers usually have and offer a selling process that is proactive and focused on creating a competitive environment for the seller. In other words, they try to play off one potential buyer against another with the goal of maximizing the dollar value of the sale. Unlike the passive process used by business brokers, the process M&A advisors and investment bankers employ tends to help elevate the sales price, so it makes sense to keep that in mind as you interview prospective firms.

Most M&A advisors and investment bankers will put together a thick book about a business—one that's full of details about every aspect of the company—and send it out to all the potential strategic and institutional buyers. Often they will do so with a deadline to receive sealed bids and offers. The process can take a while, perhaps up to a year, but a firm that understands the market for a particular type of business and knows what it's doing will be worth every penny of the commission it's paid because it will be able to achieve the highest selling price possible.

The Story of Dave and Marie

Now let me relate another case history of a business start-up by a man I will call Dave and his wife, Marie. The genesis of their business was the Iraq War. Dave worked for a high-tech firm that had a couple of government contracts. It happened that the U.S. Army had purchased a software system that Dave had helped develop, and he was sent to Iraq during the war to provide on-site training and support for the program. He worked in a division command post where he was able to watch the war, the occupation, and policing by the military on a big computer screen.

Dave saw firsthand how desperate people in a populated area can become when the electric grid is no longer reliable, and basic services, such as sanitation and trash removal, were no longer in operation. Whenever he and others left the base, they would fly in a Blackhawk helicopter as close as possible to the ground in order to avoid being a target for surface-to-air missiles. It gets very hot in Iraq, and sometimes it would be 120-130 degrees Fahrenheit outside. They flew with the doors wide open and Dave could look down and see what conditions were like on the ground for the people of Bagdad. Trash was everywhere, and it smelled so bad it would take his breath away.

The United States military was doing all it could do to improve the situation and to restore services, but it became clear to

Dave that if a foreign military ever invaded the United States, it would be fairly easy for them to use food and water, the electric grid, roads, and telecom infrastructure to exercise control. And it wasn't just an invasion by a foreign power that Dave began to worry about. Nowadays, so much depends on the electric grid, the ability to transport goods, and communications—from Just-in-Time inventory, to interstate and intercontinental travel and transportation—that without the massive infrastructure required, civilization would rapidly dissolve in to chaos and mayhem. To put it simply, people would not be able to drive to Wal-Mart and swipe their credit cards to get food.

According to a 2008 report by the U.S. Senate Committee on Homeland Security & Governmental Affairs, if something knocked out the electric grid for an extended period, such as an electromagnetic pulse (EMP) caused by the explosion at high altitude of a nuclear device by a rogue nation like Iran or North Korea, a natural disaster like the Hurricane in Puerto Rico in September 2017, or a computer hacking operation by a hostile foreign power like Russia or China, millions of people would die from hunger, from starvation, from lack of water, and from social disruption. One estimate by the U.S. government says that after a year 90 percent of the population would be dead.

A few years after he returned from Iraq, Dave met and married Marie, a marketing executive for a large company. He did his best not to think about the horror he had witnessed during the Iraq War and occupation, but it did stay in the back of his mind. Dave and Marie both liked the peace and quiet of the countryside, and so they moved some distance from the city where they both worked to a house they bought that got its water from a well. During a power outage caused by an ice storm, Dave was reminded of his time in Bagdad. Without electricity, a twenty-first century well doesn't work, and so no water comes into the house, and that means no shower, no washing dishes, and no flushing toilets. Dave's first impulse was to by a gasoline generator, which he did, but when he thought about it, he realized that would not be a good solution during an extended period without power from the electric utility. Not only would a generator eventually run out of gas, which might be hard to find and replace if there was no electricity, he discovered that most generators only remain under warrantee for 500 hours, which meant one would probably wear out and conk out if it had to run night and day for weeks and weeks. So, being a resourceful, high-tech sort of guy, Dave rigged up a system that used a solar panel and battery backup to run the well pump.

Then came the Great Recession of 2008-2010, which hit the company where Dave worked pretty hard, and just before 2010, he was laid off. Fortunately, Marie still had a job, but Dave needed to find employment. The more he thought, the more he remembered Bagdad and what it was like during the power outage at his home before he designed and installed the solar panel system for the well. Marie encouraged Dave to see if he could find a way to use that solar panel system as an initial building block for a company to start. So Dave put an ad on Craigslist for a solar panel system that would power a well pump, and he got a surprisingly large response. The rest, as they say, is history. Soon Dave was spending all his time creating, delivering, and installing the system he had designed. It wasn't long before he began hiring workers to help him construct and install them, and he went from self-employed to business owner. Then Dave took another big step forward and graduated to installing solar panel systems with banks of back-up batteries that could run an entire house off grid. Soon, the business was doing so well, Marie quit her job and went to work with Dave in order to put her marketing skills to work for the new firm. She was able to establish relationships with banks that were willing to make loans to homeowners that wanted to install solar systems, and she used her marketing skills to spread the word.

Today Dave and Marie have the largest company in their region of the country that's in the business of installing residential solar power systems with backup energy storage. Dave believes strongly in what he is doing because of his experience in Iraq—he sees it as his mission. He and Marie are committed to getting as many households as possible self-sufficient and energy independent. Not only that, they are convinced their customers are making a wise investment whether or not an extended power outage ever happens because their homeowner customers are able to sell the excess electricity their solar panels generate back to the local electric utility. In many months that reduces their electric bills to zero. In addition, the federal government currently offers a 30 percent tax rebate on such systems, which means that most homeowners can have a solar system without putting any money down. And since that dramatically reduces or even zeros out how much they spend each month on electricity, in many cases the payment they make on the solar system is fully offset by the reduction of their electric bills, not to mention their decreased carbon footprint. No wonder Dave and Marie's business is booming. Last year they brought in more than $6 million and their business continues growing fast.

Business Startup Possibilities

Let's say you have a job. You have spent time in a library, or some other quiet place, identifying what puts you in the zone.

You have even thought of how to put that activity to work for others in a way people will be happy to pay for. But you don't want to take a big chance and quit your job. After all, you've got to eat and you have to pay the rent. So how can you make a safe transition from job, to self-employed, to business owner?

Although Dave got laid off from his high tech firm and was forced to find something to do, an action he took might point the way. As you recall, he put an ad on Craigslist offering the well pump solar power system he had developed, and he found out there was market for it. Perhaps you could do something similar while you still have a job, or as Jim Rohn once said, "Work full-time on your job and part-time on you fortune." That way, you can test the waters safely, and if you find there is a market, ease into a transition. You might try selling a product or service on Craigslist, for example, or one of the many venues on the Internet that now exist for people looking for gigs, or to sell their wares. Then deliver the product or service during evenings or weekends or on days you don't have to work at your regular job. There are many venues you might consider using to sell a product or product line instead of, or in addition to, Craigslist.

As you think about this, it may be helpful to know that according to Ellen Lin, author of *How I Built a Million Dollar Online Store from $600,* the best products to sell online, especially through Amazon, have the following characteristics:

- They are small in size and lightweight for low-cost, easy shipping.

- They do not have an expiration date.

- They should be niche products that can only be found in a specialty store if anywhere.

- They have the potential to be built into a full product line. (The more items you have to sell, the better.)

- They do not depreciate in value over time.

Here are some URLs. Follow them to check out those that interest you:

Craigslist: https://www.craigslist.org/about/sites?lang=vi#US

You also can use Facebook Marketplace:
https://www.facebook.com/marketplace/

You can sell practically anything on eBay:
https://www.ebay.com/sl/sell

You can set up your own store on Etsy to sell what you might have to offer that's handcrafted, vintage, custom, or unique:
https://www.etsy.com/

You can also sell your product on Amazon. Amazon charges fees and has two levels with different fee structures, one for professionals and another for individuals. Follow this link to learn more:
https://services.amazon.com/selling/getting-started

My in-the-zone activity is writing. If it's yours as well, you can write books and publish them as Kindle eBooks and as trade paperbacks on Amazon, and it won't cost you a cent. Simply create and upload computer files of your books. Amazon converts Microsoft Word files to Kindle, and PDFs are used for paperbacks, which Amazon prints on demand whenever one is ordered. Follow this link to learn more:

https://kdp.amazon.com/

By the way, if you are serious about publishing books, here's a link to one that you will want to read. It's called, *HOW I SOLD 80,000 BOOKS: Book Marketing for Authors (Self Publishing through Amazon and Other Retailers):*

https://www.amazon.com/dp/B00WWUR1O4

There are also a number of ecommerce websites where you can sell services—anything from creative writing such as blogging, copywriting, or web development, mobile app development, accounting and tax preparation, or art direction and design, marketing services such as SEO, social media, email automation, or even consulting services, which might include financial planning, legal consulting, business planning, and so forth.

The big one in this field is Upwork:

https://www.upwork.com/

And here are ten additional freelance websites you might want to check out:

PeoplePerHour: https://www.peopleperhour.com/

Guru: https://www.guru.com/

Freelancer: https://www.freelancer.com/

iWriter: https://www.iwriter.com/

Fiverr: https://www.fiverr.com/

99 Designs: https://99designs.com/

TopTal: https://www.toptal.com/

DesignHill: https://www.designhill.com/

Hubstaff: https://hubstaff.com/

Boxer: https://broxer.com/

Hopefully this chapter has gotten your mental wheels turning about starting a business and how you might go about it. In the upcoming chapter we will look at how to get your head in the right place to make the leap to future millionaire.

CHAPTER FOUR: Develop the Right Attitude

As was stated at the outset of this book, anyone of average intelligence who lives in a modern, free society can become rich if he or she has sufficient time ahead to accumulate wealth and a burning desire to do so. The fact that you have read this far in this book suggests you definitely have the intelligence. Assuming you also have the desire, there is no doubt in my mind you have what it takes to become a wealthy man or woman. This chapter will explain one of the most important things you need to have or acquire in order to become rich, and it will explain how to get it if you don't already have it:

The right attitude and mindset

Some people are scripted from birth for success. Their parents were wealthy, and they were surrounded from their very first breath by wealth and the advantages it can afford. For them, a wealthy mindset is second nature. If that describes you, that's good because it's one less hurdle you have to overcome. If, however, you do not have a wealthy mindset, you need to develop one. You see, in my experience, what's inside a person's head is critically important when is comes to getting rich. Of course, it's true that rich kids probably have practical advantages beyond a wealth mindset that poor kids don't have, such as the wealthy people they know, and therefore the connections they have. Perhaps they went to more prestigious schools. Maybe they also have easier access to the capital needed to start a business. All that may be true, but the advice in this chapter and the next one is meant to help you overcome a lack of connections and capital by explaining how to become a "people magnet" that draws people to you who want to join in what your are doing and help you succeed. In order for that to happen, one thing you must do is use your willpower to adjust your thinking so that it mirrors and perhaps even improves upon what is in the minds of those so-called "privileged" individuals. In this chapter, I will explain why and how.

You may be wondering why you need to change your thinking. The answer is simple. Just ask any trained therapist. You focus upon things and take actions based on your thoughts and attitudes, and what you focus upon on expands. If you think of yourself as a victim of circumstances, you will most certainly be a victim of circumstances. If you think of yourself as rich—that you deserve to be rich because it is your birthright—with a sufficient amount of effort, you will become rich. That is, in fact, the basic message of two of the most popular self-help, get-rich books of all time: *Think, and Grow Rich* by Napoleon Hill [1883-1970] and *The Science of Getting Rich* by Wallace D. Wattles [1860-1911].

Give this some thought. You and billionaire Warren Buffett were born with the same basic equipment: a brain with huge potential. Both of you are descended from a long line that goes all the way back to the very first single-cell creature that formed in the primordial sea. Both of you are the products of evolution that took place over a mind-boggling 4.5 billion years. Other hominoids that evolved along the way branched off onto dead-end paths or developed into chimpanzees or gorillas and such. Some, like the Neanderthals, made it pretty far along the evolutionary path, but eventually could no longer hack it and became extinct when your ancestors, Homo sapiens, came along and took over their territory. But your line kept going and going. Your ancestors continued evolving until they eventually arrived at the very top of the food chain. There can be no doubt at all. You are a member of a very exclusive club—one among the most gifted and highly intelligent creatures that has ever lived.

You are the pinnacle of life on earth.

Now consider this. Your mind is fantastic. Scientists say we humans typically use only a portion of its capacity. It is the most important tool you have—an amazing tool that is very much like a garden. You can cultivate it, pull out the weeds, water it, plant the right seeds, and allow them to grow. Or you can neglect it, and let it run wild. Either way, cultivated or not, it must and it will bring forth whatever is allowed to grow in it. If no good seeds are planted in your mind and allowed to flourish, useless, destructive weeds will take over and will continue producing more of their kind. Just as a gardener or farmer cultivates his plot of land, weeding it, and growing the flowers, the fruits and the vegetables he or she wants on the dinner table, so may a person tend his or her mind, weeding out the useless and destructive thoughts and cultivating only those that have the promise of bearing delicious fruit. If such cultivation does not take place, if discipline is not exercised, the result likely will not be good because what's in your mind will eventually be what's in your world.

You may be saying to yourself that you cannot help what thoughts enter your mind, and that may be true. But you can decide which thoughts to keep and which thoughts to throw away. Over time, the outer conditions of a person's life always come to be in tune with his or her inner state. By the process of planting and cultivating positive, constructive thoughts, you will sooner or later discover that you are the master gardener of your mind—the director of your life. You will also come to understand that your thoughts shape your character, which also creates your circumstances. Ultimately, what's in your mind is your destiny. A long time ago a man named James Allen [1864-1912] wrote a book about this that I highly recommend you read called, *As a Man Thinketh*.

How Your Mind Creates Your Life

Perhaps you are not convinced that what I have just written above is true. How does what's in your mind create your life? I'll explain. As you no doubt already know, the human mind has two parts: a conscious part and a subconscious part. You have direct control over the conscious part. At present, you are causing it to read these words. The reason it is vitally important to use your willpower to control and cultivate your conscious mind is that it has power over your subconscious mind, and to a great extent, your subconscious mind is what determines your circumstances and your reality. As you go about your daily routine, your subconscious mind influences the decisions you make. As mentioned before, if you have a victim mentality, your subconscious mind may dismiss or filter out all sorts of opportunities that come your way because it determines what you notice and are attracted to out of the literally millions of things you are exposed to each day. If your subconscious is convinced you are a victim, and nothing you do can change that, it may dismiss out of hand and cause you to pass by all sorts of opportunities that might lead to success if you would only take them.

How will changing your conscious mindset from victimhood to "destined-to-be-wealthy-because-it-is-your-birthright" change this? Well, consider the phenomenon of hypnotism. The reason it works is because the hypnotist bypasses the subject's conscious mind and speaks directly to the subject's subconscious mind, and the subconscious mind has no choice but to bring about that which is communicated directly to it as fact. Why? The subconscious mind is totally subjective, meaning it cannot step outside itself and take an objective look at what is going on. As such, it is capable only of deductive reasoning, which is the kind that progresses from a cause (the conscious mind's directive) forward to its ultimate end. It does not stop to question or analyze, or think about what is "good," "bad," or "desirable." This is the sort of reasoning a sociopathic criminal might use when committing a crime. He may walk into a room, see someone counting money, and think: "I need money, so I will take his. Since the man is protecting the money, I will get rid of him. I'll shoot him. He'll drop to the floor. I will then take the money and run. I'll leave by the window."

On the other hand, the conscious mind, being objective and self-aware, is able to step outside itself. It can reason both deductively and inductively. To reason inductively is to move backward from result to cause. A police detective, for example, would arrive at the scene and begin reasoning backward in an attempt to figure out how the crime was committed and who might have done it.

The fact is that the subconscious mind is entirely under the control of the conscious (objective) mind. As a result, the subconscious will work diligently to support or to bring into reality whatever the conscious mind believes and feels is true. And let me say here that it is important that the two things—belief and feeling—be in concert. The subconscious may be even more responsive to what you feel about something than what you actually think about it. So do not just hope what you want in life will come about. *Feel* it already is. If you really feel that something must be, then it *must* be. At least, that is how the subconscious interprets it, and so the subconscious mind will go to work to bring it into reality.

Something else to know is that the subconscious mind does not understand, or perhaps it simply doesn't hear the words "no" and "not." Suppose, for example, you're a tennis player. You're in a big match, it's close, and you arrive at a crucial point. Your opponent is going to serve next, and as you pass by him at the net when changing ends, you say, "You're playing great today, Henry. Don't blow it. This is a big point coming up. Whatever you do, don't double fault."

You've started Henry worrying, and on top of that, his subconscious mind doesn't hear or understand the word "don't." All it hears is "double fault," and it takes that as a directive. Try as he might to do otherwise, Henry will double fault.

Actually, I advise you not to play such a dirty trick. As the saying goes, "What goes around, comes around," and you don't want that sort of negative behavior coming back at you. More will be written about this. The important thing to remember is that self-talk and coaching should always be framed in a positive way. Do not say to yourself, "don't double fault." Rather, you should phrase the desired outcome in a positive way, such as, "Make this one an ace!" Thoughts put into words are powerful. Positive affirming self-talk will change your life. Say to yourself and think: "I'm good, I'm wealthy, I'm the luckiest person I know!"

Think Positive and Rid Yourself of Fear

Let's dig into the issue of fear because fears are thoughts, beliefs, and feelings, and thoughts, beliefs, and feelings are what create your reality.

To learn what you fear, tune into your moment-to-moment stream of consciousness and observe what makes you worried, anxious, resentful, uptight, afraid, angry, and so on. Step outside yourself and identify unsettled emotions, tugs and urges that have become part of your programming. Slow down and consider what triggered a negative emotion. Did your temper flare? Why? Why was it so important for things to go a certain way? If you trace what you felt back to its cause, in most cases, you will come to a particular variety of fear, and it's been said that only two fears are instinctive: the fear of falling and loud noises. Other fears were acquired, and whatever was acquired can be disposed of.

According to some experts, the fears that hold people back can be grouped under one of six headings:

- the fear of poverty (or failure),
- the fear of criticism,
- the fear of ill health,
- the fear of the loss of love,
- the fear of old age,
- and the fear of death.

I will focus on the fear of poverty (failure) because it is the biggest deterrent many face when it comes to accumulating and achieving wealth. Like anything that's held in the mind long enough, it is self-fulfilling because traits develop that bring it about. For example, are you a procrastinator? An underlying fear of failure is probably the root cause and can be counted upon to produce the unwanted result.

Are you overly cautious? Do you see the negative side of every circumstance or stall for the "right time" before taking action? Do you worry that things will not work out, have doubts (generally expressed by excuses or apologies about why you probably won't be able to perform), do you suffer from indecision (which leads to someone else, or circumstances, making the decision for you)?

Are you indifferent? This generally shows itself as laziness or a lack of initiative, enthusiasm or self-control.

Step back and listen for internal voices that say "can't" or "don't" or "won't" or "too risky" or "why bother?"

How do you get rid of them? Shoo them away.

No matter who you are—president, king, or knave—the only thing over which you have absolute control is your thoughts. As was stated earlier, you may not be able to control what thoughts enter your mind, but you can decide whether to discard one or to keep it. Thoughts are not part of you, and that means you can decide that a thought is counterproductive and throw it away, or you can turn it over and over in your mind, in effect nurture it, and let it grow. You are who you are and what you are, and what you will become, because of your thoughts. Make them productive.

If negative thinking is a problem for you, go to YouTube and find hypnotic meditations to listen to that will plant positive thoughts in your mind in place of negative ones. Play them over and over for at least a month. Get all that junk out of your head. One I recommend is "Money & Success - Bedtime Guided Meditation" by Barry Tesar. You can find it on YouTube.

Until you started reading this book, you may have thought you were at the mercy of conditions outside yourself, that you have either been lucky or unlucky, and that chance has brought you where you are today. That is not true. You have brought yourself to this place, and most likely, you did it unconsciously. If it's not where you want to be, you have arrived here because of programming that took place when you were a child. Now that you know this, it's time to reprogram yourself.

The Power of Positive Thinking

I suspect you have heard about "The Power of Positive Thinking," that positive thoughts are much more likely to produce good results than negative thoughts. I'm reminded of *The Little Engine That Could,* an American fairy tale published numerous times in illustrated children's books and movies since its original debut in 1930. The Little Engine was a railroad locomotive that was tasked with pulling a long, heavy train—one that seemed much too large for it—up and over a mountain. But even so, the Little Engine was determined and kept telling itself over and over, "I think I can, I think I can." It was a struggle, but the Little Engine persevered and finally succeeded.

It's a good story and a valuable one to teach young children the benefits of optimism and hard work. The problem is, many of us today were not taught that lesson as children, and in fact, feelings of frustration, discontent, and dissatisfaction were ways of solving problems that many of us "learned" as infants. For example, if a baby is hungry, he or she expresses discontent by crying. Lo and behold, a warm and tender hand appears magically out of nowhere and brings a bottle of milk. Later on, if the baby is uncomfortable, again, he or she will again express dissatisfaction, and the same warm, comforting hands magically appear and solve the problem. That's fine for babies but, unfortunately, many children continue to get their way and have their problems solved by indulgent parents merely by continuing to express their feelings of frustration when things don't work the way they want. All they have to do is feel frustrated and dissatisfied, express their dissatisfaction, and the problem will be solved. Sometimes what have become known as "helicopter parents" continue to cater to their children in this way all the way through high school, college, and beyond.

This way of life "works" for infants, and for some children. But it does not work in adult life when a person is out in the world on his or her own. Yet many continue to expect, perhaps unconsciously, that it will work. They seem to think that by feeling discontented and expressing their grievances—if only they feel put upon enough—life, or someone will take pity on them, rush to their aid and solve their problems. Let me assure you that 99.99 percent of the time that is not going to happen. It is my advice that you take responsibility for every aspect of your life.

Imagine, for example, you are lucky enough to land an entry-level job as a management trainee in a big corporation. With you in training are several other bright young men and women fresh out of business school. Imagine the way things work in this company is often not to your liking. Management trainees, for example, are relegated to cubicles with five-foot-high walls affording little or no privacy, while the senior staff all have corner offices with large windows and spectacular views of the East River. You spend a good deal of time grumbling to yourself and to others about this injustice, subconsciously believing that will get you out of that cubicle and into a corner suite. Your fellow trainees, on the other hand, spend their time making positive suggestions and anticipating and providing for the needs of customers as well as for fellow workers higher up on the corporate ladder. Whom do you suppose is most likely to be first to break out of his or her cubicle? The one who constantly complained? Or the one that consistently delivered the goods?

Don't you feel a twinge inside that intuitively "knows" the positive attitude, the attitude of service to others, will inevitably win the day? That "twinge" is a message from something inside you that knows the correct answer called "intuition."

If you have been ignoring that feeling when it comes, now is the time for you to begin recognizing such messages. They have a light and airy feeling to them, even though they may seem to run counter to egocentric notions, such as, "The first order of business is to look out for number one." That egocentric notion may work in the short term, but in the long term, it is bad advice. The fact is that it's always best to under-promise and over-deliver to customers and bosses—as well as to anyone else for that matter. By over-delivering, your reputation grows as you create positive vibes and positive opinions of you by those with whom you come in contact. A reputation that you are someone who can be counted on can only lead to good outcomes and opportunities for you in the long run.

Let's consider for a moment why some people may spend their valuable time on earth grumbling and complaining away opportunities to get ahead. It's often because they have felt frustrated and defeated for so long—ever since they were babies in a crib and while growing up with indulgent parents—that those feelings have become ingrained. Their minds are in a kind of holding pattern, and it's never occurred to them to step outside of themselves in order to get in touch with intuition that would tell them, if they would only listen, that grumbling and complaining are counterproductive and accomplish nothing. Until they wise up, they will continue—to their own detriment—to radiate those feelings, and as sure as night follows day, their discontent will lead to failure.

No matter what your mindset, if you want to change it, it's important to know that thoughts and feelings are intertwined. It might be said that feelings are the soil in which thoughts and ideas grow. If you are habitually grumpy and in a bad mood, you need to lighten up and begin seeing the glass half full. Moreover, when you begin working toward a goal, try thinking how you will feel when you reach it—and then actually make yourself feel that way. I'm serious. Conjure up the feeling of "Success!" The thrill of accomplishment will communicate the belief to your subconscious mind that it's inevitable you are going to achieve what you have set out to accomplish. The feeling creates the belief, and the belief creates the feeling. A mental model of success will be etched into your subconscious, and that the desired outcome will surely come about.

Let's say you are pursuing a challenge and fervently want to accomplish it. Assuming you have the education, the knowledge, and the qualifications required to reach your goal, and assuming you feel strongly about it at an emotional level, you will almost certainly realize success. It's as though you are a magnet, drawing what you need to you. The greater your desire, the more powerfully your subconscious will mind work to produce results.

Be Likable and Appealing to Others

Becoming rich will require effort and work, and that means things will be easier if you have help along the way. The most likely source of that help will be friends, partners, and mentors. Obviously, the going will be easier and you will attract more help if people like you and want to work with you. Therefore, it should go without saying that it's important to be someone others want to be around—someone people would like and want as a friend. That means you need to be someone who "talks the talk," and "walks the walk." Perhaps you know a person who does the opposite. If not, you are likely to come across someone like that in your business dealings, so be prepared and never, ever be one of them. In public such people talk openly—some even brag and boast—about the importance of having integrity and doing the right thing. But in private it's a different story. They bad mouth people and do things that aren't consistent with the honest-John public persona they hope to project. People quickly see through these phonies. As the old saying goes, "Say what you mean, and mean what you say," and people will respect you for doing so.

This is not to say you shouldn't be competitive. You definitely should have a competitive attitude, and of course you should enjoy the thrill of victory. It's important to have a winning attitude, winning surely beats the alternative, and very important, people want to go with a winner—they want to "hitch their wagon to a star." But it's also important to understand that you should not gloat about winning. Be humble, and realize that often a surprisingly big a payoff will come in the form of goodwill if you are a gracious loser. It is far better to give credit to others, especially where credit is due. Unless your name is Muhammad Ali [1942-2016]—the champion boxer known for his colorful bragging and boasting—never brag or boast. Such behavior indicates immaturity and insecurity.

Obey the Laws of Physics

Earlier, I wrote, "What goes around comes around." It's true and something you always ought to keep in mind. In the East, it's called "Karma." In reality, it is simply "cause and effect." In fact, it's a law of physics—Newton's Third Law of Motion: "For every action, there is an equal and opposite reaction." Throw a rock into a pond, and you will disturb the harmony of the pond. You were the cause, and the effect was the splash. The ripples flow out, and they flow back until harmony is restored. In the same way, disharmonious actions by a person go out into the world and come back upon back upon that person until harmony is restored.

That is why it is always best to "live and let live," and to follow the Golden Rule, which everyone knows is to "do unto others as you would have others do unto you."

Let's dig a little deeper into this. If "what goes around comes around," the more you give, the more you will receive. In other words, what you send out into the world will return to you. Therefore, the more you assist others, in the long run, the more assistance will come to you. And it's important do it not for your own gain but because it is who you are. It is what is right. It is not some theoretical, do-gooder idea. It will work in your day-to-day life, provided your motive is to help others without seeking or expecting anything in return because, as has been said, nobody likes a phony—so don't be someone who is hoping to score brownie points in order to receive something in exchange. Be your best, unselfish self!

All well and good, you say, but what if such benevolence is not in my nature? Here's my advice: Change your nature. Absolutely do not expect anything in return and force yourself to "fake it until you feel it." As you do good deeds and see how your actions affect others, you will eventually come to enjoy doing them. In time, you will want to help others because it will make you feel good to do so. Get to know yourself. The nice thing about being human is we get to choose the person we want to be. Choose characteristics that make you proud, proud of everything about you.

Let's say you are in business and someone lashes out at you in anger. What should you do? Say, for example, you're the owner of a business and a competitor or vendor files a lawsuit against your business based on some real or perceived grievance. Rather than strike back and escalate the problem, the first thing to do is to gather the facts. Get everyone from your company together who knows anything about the vendor and what may actually have happened to cause the dispute. The group should do its best to determine what really happened and come up with all of the issues and interests the other side may have.

Such questions ought to be answered such as, "What can we do to get them what they want or need?" To persuade them to withdraw the suit, you might decide to offer to them a contract or an attractive benefit in some other area of the business or part of the country. Your objective is to restore harmony rather than provoke and escalate chaos. Finding a win-win solution often can do just that. You and your group will probably want to brainstorm and evaluate the effects different actions will have on the specific individuals bringing suit. What does the leader of the other side want, personally?

The bottom line is that you can get into a back-and-forth fight that might end up harming your business as well as the other guy's, or instead, by making a peace offering, you might be able to mitigate the situation. In most cases, if you are gracious toward others, you will defuse what could turn into a much worse situation. It has been said that if you want to make a friend, you must be a friend.

Of course there are unreasonable individuals in this world, and there are bullies who refuse to be placated. Sometimes people will sue for no good reason at all, except that they want to get something for nothing. Often such individuals understand only one thing, and that's a punch in the nose—figuratively speaking, of course. If that's the case, do what you have to do, but only after an attempt at reasoning with them. The figurative punch in the nose should be used only as a last resort. The point is that things are more likely to fall into place for you if you are able to establish and maintain harmony with others. And, happily, the benefits do not stop with simply falling into place.

Be a Strong Leader and Build a Great Team

The success of a business enterprise typically comes as a result of the skills, attitudes, and actions of everyone down the line pulling together to move forward. But even though dedication and skill are requisites for success, talented and capable employees aren't all that's needed to win. Something else is equally important. This something is what harnesses the available energy and talent and channels it toward a goal. It's what will create a great team that consistently outperforms its competition. Whether it's a sports team, a school class, or a business, for the highest level of effectiveness to be reached, what's needed is solid and consistent leadership. Even a team comprised of outstanding individuals can falter unless a leader gets them working together in harmony. You can probably think of a few professional sports teams that have a lot of talent but still never seem to make the playoffs.

Much has been written about leadership, but it seems to me that leadership can be boiled down to a single core attribute—a leader's personal commitment to the company, the team, or the objective everyone has bought into. That commitment is what encourages people to follow. Personal commitment compels an individual to take the necessary actions and to have the courage to follow through and persevere until the goal is reached. Personal commitment aligns the thoughts and minds of the leader and the team so that the sum is greater than the parts and even unconscious actions lead toward positive results. Moreover, personal commitment breeds the most important ingredient of all, a bond of trust between team members and the leader, trust that the actions to be taken will lead to the best result. Think about it. People may respect another person's intellect but at the same time sense that the individual is not committed. And like it our not, most people simply are not going to follow someone they don't trust.

Many types of leaders exist, but it seems to me the trait they all share is commitment to an endeavor, an organization, or a goal. This is needed in order to have the courage and tenacity to continue ahead through tough times. To those around them, such commitment is self-evident and leads to a high level of trust among followers. Team members know they can count on their leader to show the way. They are led by example. The leader will reinforce his team's trust by taking responsibility when misfortune occurs.

Giving Credit to Others Builds Loyalty

Rather than take credit for achievements, great leaders build loyalty on top of trust by giving credit where credit is due—and perhaps sometimes even when it is not due. Ronald Reagan, for example, almost never took credit for the achievements of his administration, but instead was quick to praise his staff. In doing so he achieved a high level of loyalty among his followers.

What else is a great leader able to do? He or she is able to articulate a vision the team can easily grasp. For Reagan it was his "Shining City on a Hill." The leader points the way for the team to proceed to realization of the vision and in doing so generates optimism and bolsters belief the goal can be reached. And, as has been said, "Everything is possible for one who believes." (Mark 9:23 NIV)

Other Qualities of Great Leaders

Typically, great leaders are good listeners. They want to know what others think, and do not believe they, themselves, always have the best or right answer. They are smart enough to use the intelligence and the experience of others, and understand a good idea can come from anywhere at any time and from anyone. When a great leader comes in contact with an idea that makes sense, he or she recognizes and heeds the sensation of truth that resonates within. You might say the idea or thought seems to "click." Timid or unsure individuals often will dismiss that feeling. Great leaders are secure with themselves. They see when someone else has a better idea, and they have the self-confidence to put that idea to work.

Great leaders also are demanding. They simply do not tolerate mediocrity. This may be one of the most difficult roles to play because it's human nature to want others to like you, and if you push people hard, they may not like it—or you. Nevertheless, great leaders review and evaluate, and demand improvement and excellence. William Welch at General Electric was reported to be a master at this and had the reputation of constantly having driven his subordinates to the pinnacle of excellence. Vince Lombardi, Winston Churchill, and Louis Gerstner of IBM all used high expectations to achieve goals. They were willing to make the tough decisions and to bring them to reality.

Great leaders have and show respect for the people they lead, whether they are soldiers, employees, players, or citizens. They lead by example and by doing so demonstrate they are worthy of being followed. They are personally committed to the institution they head, as well as the objectives of the institution, and are out front personally doing whatever they can to reach it.

A man I know who took over a company during a troubled time and led it out of the woods to achieve great success told me he learned something important about leadership when he hired a few executives who came highly recommended by others in his industry. They had great contacts and used them. They were also very articulate, intelligent, and from all appearances accomplished executives. But, once on board, the people who reported to them saw through them. The problem was, they viewed their new company as a stepping-stone to bigger jobs down the road—a weigh station on a carefully mapped out route. Team members picked up on this and refused to follow them. They knew, perhaps without fully articulating it, who was looking out for number one, and who was committed. This made the road a rough one—the teams questioning the commitment of their leaders.

Leading by Example

For everyone to pull together for success, executives need to roll up their sleeves and get their hands dirty right next to their employees. They need to be visible and involved, rather than aloof and apart. The goal is for everyone to feel a sense of equality, that they are members of the same team regardless of the title that follows their names. One way to help create this is to eliminate all perks. Like it our not, executives will always be paid more than other employees. It makes sense they should be paid in proportion to the time they must devote, the risks they must take, and the expectations placed on them. But pay is one thing, and perks are another. It works against a healthy atmosphere to set executives apart, or to place them on a pedestal by giving them perks and other special treatment. That's why it makes sense to eliminate executive perks. No fancy offices, no limos, no reserved parking spots, and no exotic meeting locations.

Employees are not blind. They see what's going on. They watch the executives closely and determine for themselves if each one is "walking the talk." Face it. Employees quickly figure out which leaders are personally committed and which are not. They know which ones are only looking out for number one, and they respond to and follow the leaders accordingly.

Always Keep Your Life in Balance

You are probably familiar with the ancient Chinese symbol composed of a white "yin" interlocking a black "yang" that represents dual nature of things. It symbolizes that we live in a world that is composed of opposites: Up, down, black, white, good and evil. Without the tension opposites create, nothing would or could exist—everything would fall apart. Follow the advice of this book and attain total success but do not allow complacency to set in. Always seek new challenges, realizing that without one, self-destruction may be the result. By keeping success and challenge in balance, it will be possible to maintain your position and retain your success.

It can also be comforting to know there can be no growth without at least some discontent. Deep within, you know what is best for you. There is an urge built into you that pushes you to strive for growth, and for most of us, growth will not continue without some agitation and discontent. So study your dissatisfactions. They will tell you what you are about to leave behind and possibly point you in a new direction. Be willing to be uncomfortable. It is the only way you grow.

As you contemplate your future course, it is also important to realize you can only attract that which you feel worthy of. Self-esteem is critical to success. The truth is you are not what you have, and you are not simply what you do. Beneath your fear programming, you are a magnificent creature composed of billions of living, conscious cells. To repeat what was written earlier, you are the pinnacle of life on Earth. Fear and negative programming are all that can prevent you from realizing your full potential. The more you can let go of the fears, the higher your self esteem will be, and the more options you will have and the more risks you can take. The more you like yourself, the more others will like you, and the more worthy you will feel.

You can have anything you want if you can give up the belief you cannot have it and replace it with the belief you can. Of course, you must get the education necessary and learn the skills you need to create what you want. "Where your attention goes, your energy flows." You attract what you are and that which you concentrate upon. If you are negative, you draw in and experience negativity. If you have a loving attitude toward others, you draw in and experience love. You can attract to yourself only those qualities you possess. So, if you want peace and harmony in your life, you must become peaceful and harmonious. If you want wealth, you must develop a wealthy attitude.

The mind is engaged in an endless state of growth and reorganization. This is good because it means you can discard old, negative-thought baggage and replace it with productive thoughts and ideas. You might think of yourself as the pilot of a speedboat. The boat is your mind, and you can steer it in any direction you want. The wake behind the boat is your past, and good or bad, there's no reason to look back because you are headed for a bright future up ahead. It is absolutely true that it is possible to reprogram yourself. It can be done, as mentioned previously, by repeatedly listening to success-meditation recordings, or with visualization techniques. If you feel anxiety in crowds, for example, imagine yourself feeling relaxed while in a crowd of people. If you are nervous about public speaking, imagine yourself calmly addressing a crowd of adoring fans that want nothing more than to hear what you have to say. Practice the skill over and over until you create a new self-image for yourself.

Finally, when considering your new challenge, your path to riches, you may want to consider whether it is something you will do alone, or if it can be more readily accomplished in cooperation with others. When two or more people of similar purpose come together to accomplish that purpose, their combined energy directed toward the attainment of it is doubled, tripled, quadrupled, or more. The prolific author of personal-success literature, Napoleon Hill called attention to the advantages of this in his perennial bestseller, *Think, and Grow Rich*. It is definitely something worth considering. In my case, I partnered with my older brother, and as previously mentioned, we brought in highly capable people as partners and key executives. We formed a team that became an industry juggernaut, and we ended up selling the business for ten times earnings—a practically unheard of high multiple.

Take Time to Make a Life

Perhaps you have heard the saying, "Never become so busy making a living that you do not have time to make a life." That's advice worth taking that should start with doing what's necessary to maintain a healthy balance between your work life and your home life. If you are married, for example, pay attention to your spouse. Keep the romance that brought you together going strong. If you have children, spend time with each one of them. Listen to them. Take them to lunch or to an amusement park. Ask them questions. Coach their little league teams. Constantly give them encouragement. Attend their recitals. Applaud their successes. The fact is you have within you everything required for your life to become a virtual paradise if you choose to accept that it is possible, if you have the desire to make it so, and if you maintain a healthy balance in all areas of your life. We live in a world of abundance, although many populating our planet appear to view it as a universe of scarcity. Too bad for them, but it does not have to be so for you.

What else might you do to maintain balance and thereby create a happier life? Here are a few suggestions:

- Take five minutes, twice a day to affirm your goals, dreams, and desires. Most of us do not achieve our goals, not because we are too lazy or not talented enough, but because we forget about them and focus our efforts elsewhere.
- Spend some time in nature. Even if it is just ten minutes a day, take the time to go for a short walk or sit in a place surrounded by the natural world. Release the stress of the day by communing with Mother Nature, and you will soon feel recharged.
- Exercise. Your body is your temple and your most important possession. Take care of it. If it is not in top form, neither will you be in top form. Exercising, eating healthy and taking care of your amazing vehicle is vitally important for you to be able to produce at the highest levels.
- Take time to meditate. The biggest improvements in our lives almost always come from within. An effective way to release the limiting beliefs and destructive thoughts that may plague you is to meditate for fifteen to thirty minutes a day. Regular practice of meditation has been proven scientifically to change your brain chemistry, lower blood pressure, help you sleep better, feel less stressed, and more.
- Smile a lot. A smile can change the world. Not only for you but also for the people with whom you interact. Prac-

tice a genuine smile and give joy to the world. Impact the world today and every day by smiling at everyone that passes by.
- Find more ways to have fun. Life does not have to be a strict, gloomy experience we struggle through. Instead it can be full of amazing twists and turns. Think of it as an adventure because that's what it is. Approach it as such.
- Make sure you laugh out loud at least once a day. Do something childish, or completely weird. Be yourself, have fun, and laugh at your own jokes.
- Remember that everything begins as a thought or idea. Ideas and experiences create beliefs that in turn, create your reality. If you are not satisfied with your current reality, you must change your beliefs and your behavior. Beliefs should be changed when you realize which ones are not working for you. Change that belief, and your life will change.

I'll finish this chapter with this thought. To change for the better, you must first recognize the destructive or disharmonious thinking and behavior you need to eliminate. Understand that you don't have to change how you feel about it, you simply need to change what you are doing. The Buddha was right when he said, "It is your resistance to what is that causes your suffering." By suffering, he meant everything that doesn't work in your life. This might include relationship problems, loss of loved ones, loneliness, sickness, accidents, guilt, financial hardship, unfulfilled desires, and so on. When you accept what you cannot change, you will be in position to set that aside and stop worrying about it. And yes, you absolutely should change what you are able to change that needs changing—no doubt about it. But you also need to have the wisdom to accept what you cannot change. Out of acceptance will come detachment, which will enable you to enjoy the positive aspects of life without being distracted by the negative. Why waste energy focusing on things from the past when you can move on and put those things behind you? Remember, you are the pilot of the speedboat.

I'm reminded of something my mom told me many times when I was growing up, "If at first you don't succeed, try, try again." That phrase became imprinted on my brain, and I'm glad it did because it is one of the most important keys to success. Thomas Edison, for example, conducted 10,000 experiments before he found a way to make an incandescent light bulb that actually worked for a substantial length of time. When asked how it felt to fail 10,000 times, he replied, "I didn't fail. I found 10,000 ways not to make a light bulb." For him, every failure was a small success bringing him closer to accomplishing his goal. The same can be true for you if you decide to look at life that way. You and you alone are responsible for everything that happens to you. Take full responsibility for every aspect of you life. All is a result of your past thoughts, words, and deeds, which have formed your present attitude. Your attitude toward life and your experiences are returned to you as love and joy, or as confusion, trouble, and heartbreaking experiences. The way to mitigate the punishments is to take total responsibility for your life, grow in wisdom with each new life lesson, and seek harmony in everything you do.

Now that you have your mind in the right place, in the next chapter we will explore how to begin to build your brand.

CHAPTER FIVE: Be Conscious of and Build Your Brand

My brother, David N. Martin [1930-2012], co-founder of The Martin Agency, defined a brand as, "a name that stands for something—one that conveys an expectation of performance." He might ask, for example, what comes to mind when someone says the word, "Mercedes?"

How about: "Volvo . . . Porsche . . . or Volkswagen?"

"Starbucks?"

"Amazon?"

Those are brands that stand for something. They convey an expectation of performance, and I'll bet as you read each one, you either felt good about it—that it's a brand that's fit for you—or that it is not a fit.

If you accept David's definition, some people's names are brands. What do you think when you hear:

"Donald Trump?"
"Bernie Sanders?"
"Taylor Swift?"
"Justin Bieber?"
"Winston Churchill?"
"George Patton?"
"LeBron James?"
"Mahatma Gandhi?"
"Tiger Woods?"

Now, here's the important question: What do you want people to think when they hear your name?

If you answered, "A mover and shaker—the go-to person in his or her field—who is genuinely a good guy or gal and fun to work with," then follow the advice in Chapter Four. That's what will make you into someone people want to work with and be around. There can be no doubt about it. A good reputation is worth more than money can buy so make sure that's what you develop and maintain through the actions you take and the ways you conduct yourself. It will pay to guard your reputation. Choose the right friends and associates. Be of great character, keep your word and do the right things. Follow that advice and you cannot go wrong.

That having been said, this chapter is about how to get the word out about your personal brand as well as your product or company brand. In other words, it's about marketing yourself and your company once you have decided that you would like to become a business owner. For the techniques about to be discussed to work, however, it cannot be over emphasized that it's vitally important that you and your product or company be authentic—the real deal. Something marketing executives agree on is that, "Nothing kills a bad product (brand) faster than good advertising." What they mean by that is that advertising or communications may cause people to try your product or your company—but as was said a couple of times already, "Nobody likes a phony." That means you and your business must deliver on the promise and the image projected by your communications, or people will drop you and your product like a hot potato.

How to Create a Brand Image for Yourself & Your Company

As soon as you have a plan in place to move forward to self-employment and eventually to become a business owner, it's time to begin creating a presence online if you haven't started doing so already. What turns up now when you Google your name? That's what people who hear about you are going to do—Google your name.

Are you on LinkedIn, Facebook, Instagram, and so forth? What do your social media sites say about you? If they don't reflect the real you and the image you want to project, they need to be changed so that they do.

Do you have a website? If not, you need one, and what people see there and learn from it needs to reflect the authentic you. Everything people will see online when they Google your name needs work together to tell your story because more than anything, your story is what creates your brand image.

Let's talk about the value of a good story. Remember Dave? You read about him in Chapter Three—the man who created a solar panel installation company because he saw what people went through in Iraq when the electric grid was down. He worried that it could happen here. Doing something about that possibility became his cause, his story, and the basis of his brand. If you were to Google Dave's name or the name of his company, that's what you would find on the company's website, Dave's LinkedIn and Facebook pages.

Recently, Dave has written and published a book about what he saw in Iraq, the very real threat our society faces because of our dependence on the electric grid, and how, as a result, he designed and had a house built for himself and his family that is capable of operating totally off the grid. That's right. He and Marie now have children, and they live in a house Dave designed and built that can run independently from all public utilities, including electric, gas, water and sewer. The system Dave designed and developed will heat, cool, and run all the twenty-first century appliances anyone could possibly want for a full year or more. Dave's book explains how it was done and how, in the long run, it won't cost any more than a normal house because of the savings he and Marie enjoy from having virtually eliminated their utility bills. The implication, of course, is that Dave and his company can do the same for anyone who is interested.

Dave is not the only person to use a book to help build a personal brand and create an image. Consider the following:

- John F. Kennedy: *Profiles in Courage*
- Donald Trump: *The Art of the Deal*
- Stephen Covey: *The 7 Habits of Highly Effective People*
- Hillary Clinton: *It Takes a Village*
- Barack Obama: *Dreams from My Father,* and *The Audacity of Hope*
- Bernie Sanders: *Our Revolution*
- David Ogilvy: *Confessions of an Advertising Man*
- Michelle Obama: *Becoming*

Maybe you should write a book, or hire a ghostwriter to write one for you. I've ghostwritten and published several books that have greatly benefited my clients and their businesses. The books contained their ideas and knowledge. I was simply the wordsmith who was able to put what they wanted to say down on paper and get it out to the public.

How to Market Yourself and Your Product or Service

You probably think people will choose you and your product or service if you give them enough good reasons to do so—such as lots of features and benefits and a completive price—but that's only partly true. Marketing professionals will tell you there are different types of purchase decisions. There are high-commitment and low-commitment purchases and considered (i.e., highly rational) and impulse (i.e., highly emotional) decisions. The working assumption is that impulse decisions usually correlate with low-commitment purchases and considered decisions with high-commitment purchases.

After all, it's only rational, right? The problem is, we human beings usually aren't as rational as we like to think we are. Otherwise, why would a woman spend hours agonizing over which shade of lipstick or eye shadow to buy? Doesn't that fall into the low-commitment purchase category? And why would a real-estate agent go through the trouble of baking cookies in the oven when showing a house to prospective buyers? Buying a house is the biggest financial decision most people make in their lifetimes. It should be a highly rational, deeply considered one. Yet the emotional stimulus of the aroma of cookies baking can create a subliminal feeling about a place that can override rationality.

The fact is that except for the character in *Star Trek,* Dr. Spock—who was only half human—nobody makes totally rational decisions. What this means is that facts about your brand are important to your audience, but only secondarily. People make purchase decisions—all kinds of decisions for that matter—on the basis of emotion, and then look for facts and rational arguments to justify their emotional decision.

If you don't believe this, just ask University of Virginia psychology professor Jonathan Haidt, or read his 2012 book, *The Righteous Mind: Why Good People are Divided by Politics and Religion.* In a massive survey, Haidt found that people are fundamentally intuitive, not rational. The fact is that if you want to persuade others, you have to appeal to their sentiments. We humans were never designed to listen to reason. When researchers asked people moral questions and then timed their responses and scanned their brains, their answers and brain activation patterns indicated that they reached conclusions quickly and afterward produced reasons to justify what they had already decided.

The problem isn't that people don't reason. They do reason. But their arguments aim to support their conclusions, which may be very different from your conclusion or my conclusion. Reason doesn't work like a judge, impartially weighing evidence or guiding us to wisdom. It works more like a lawyer or a public relations professional, justifying our acts and judgments to others. That's why you need more than facts and figures and a rational argument to sell your brand.

You need a good story as well—one that evokes emotion.

We Each Have a Story to Tell

It seems to me that if you dig deeply enough, just about very person, every company, every brand has a story, and telling that tale can create a bond with potential customers. The truth is that almost all compelling stories boil down to the same essential plot, as was pointed out years ago by a professor at Sarah Lawrence College, Joseph Campbell [1904-1987]. He explained this in a book, *The Hero with a Thousand Faces,* first published in 1949. He pointed out that the same basic story has been told time and again in different cultures across the world, throughout recorded history and probably before. You can see it plainly in fairy tales and myths. He called it, "The Hero's Journey."

Consider Jack in "Jack and the Beanstalk," and Dorothy in "The Wizard of Oz," as examples. A sympathetic character—the hero—ventures from his or her everyday world into a place or region unlike any he or she has known before. Forces are encountered there that attempt to destroy the hero, but the hero perseveres and pushes forward in what may at times seem like a lost cause. Even so, after a great struggle, and a dark moment when all seems lost, a decisive victory is won. The hero then returns home in possession of the elixir and lives happily ever after.

Jack, for example, went to the giant's castle; Dorothy to the Land of Oz. Jack brought back the magic harp that returned harmony and prosperity to the kingdom where he lived, which had been in terrible disarray before he left. Dorothy brought back to the farm in Kansas the knowledge and understanding that there's, "No place like home."

Dave's story is similar. His journey took him to the war in Iraq. His dark moment came when he lost his job, but he pushed forward and discovered the path to victory was the solar panel system he had developed to run his well pump. Often, the elixir takes the form of knowledge or newly acquired understanding that translates into power or opportunity the hero can share with the people of his community. This is true of Dave's story, and that understanding, coupled with the humble solar panel, allows him to virtually eliminate the threat we all face from the possibility of a hacked electric grid, or one destroyed by an EMP.

This tale—"The Hero's Journey"—creates a bond between the reader or viewer and the protagonist (you or your brand) because it is a story everyone can relate to. If you think about it, our lives tend to be one hero's journey after another. It might be that our car breaks down on a country road miles from home, or we lose our job, or we are diagnosed with a life-threatening disease. We humans typically face a series of trials and tribulations—Hero's Journeys—as the years role by. Eventually, most of them work out, and we return home with the elixir—which most often is that we are wiser and more evolved than when we left. That's why we root for and identify with others who have faced and overcome difficult situations.

Most likely there is something unique, something special in your life that has pushed you, or is pushing you, to want to go into business for yourself. For me, it was my love of the act of creating, and storytelling, and that the writing process puts me in the zone. I can work at a keyboard for hours and yet it only seems like minutes because I become so absorbed in what I am doing. Whatever the underlying motivation is in your case, it is the reason you do whatever you do—the basis of a story that can be the springboard to a compelling brand image. It is what—perhaps figuratively speaking—will bring customers to your door and will set your company apart, giving it a "Core Identity." Whenever that core identity is known, understood, and practiced day in and day out by the leadership and staff of an organization, a powerful signal is sent to the world outside that can work like a magnet to attract customers.

What's Your Story?

Here are some questions to ask yourself to help you put your finger on you or your company's story:

- What drives or motivates you? Why did you decide to start the company?
- What happened to create that drive or cause that decision?
- Why do people want to help or work with you?
- When someone outside hears your name, or the organization's name, what do you suppose comes to mind? Or, if you haven't yet built an image, what would you like to have come to mind?
- What do you, or will this organization do better than any other?
- If you or the organization were to cease to exist, what would be lost as a result?
- Looking forward, what do you wish to achieve [in addition to becoming wealthy]?
- What is your image or reputation today?
- What do people like most about what you do, or what your company does?
- What would your organization be like five years from now if you could wave a magic wand and make it happen?
- What must be done for you and the organization to prosper into the future?
- If a story about you or the organization were to appear on TV or in newspapers five years from now, what would you like the headline or logline to say?
- What do you believe to be the best single word to describe your organization and what it offers? For example, can the company's story be summed up in a single word such as, "Reliability?" "Safety?" "Variety?" "Fun?" "Value?" "Security?"

For Dave and Marie's solar panel company, it's "Security." In other words, their customers know that they and their families will be able to survive comfortably even if the electric grid goes down and stays down for an extended period of time. "Security" is their company's core identity—their company's "One Thing." What do the answers to the questions above boil down to in your case? What's your "One Thing?"

The Four Ps of Marketing

Let's dig deeper in our effort to help you define your future business. If you have ever taken a course in marketing, you know the discipline is based on what your professor called "the Four Ps." Thinking about them in light of the company you may be planning to create can help you develop a brand and marketing strategy. Let's take a look:

Product (or Service)
Place (where sold or how distributed)
Price
Promotion

Product

- First is your product or service—what it is that you have to sell. In your case, what does the customer want? What needs does your product or service satisfy? What features does it have to meet these needs?
- How, where, and when will the customer use it?
- Do you have or will you have competitors? What do they do, and what can we learn from them?

- How can your product be differentiated? What makes it better than the competition?

Price

- Concerning price, what is the value of the product or service to the buyer?
- Are there established price points for products or services in this arena?
- How does the price of the product you are contemplating compare with that of competitive products?
- What's the best way to deliver true value to your customers? Are costly features included the customer won't actually use? Can anything be eliminated to make it less expensive?
- Is the customer price sensitive? Will a small decrease in price result in extra market share? Will a small increase not make much difference, and so result in a higher profit margin?
- What discounts should be offered to trade customers, or to other specific segments of the market?
  What is the most your product or service can cost and still provide what's needed and desired, but still be sold at a profit?

Place

- When it comes to place, where do (or will) potential buyers look for your product or service?
- If they are likely to look for it in a store, what kind of store? Will it be a specialist boutique or a supermarket, a big box, or all of the above?

- Will your customers look online? They are likely to get their information there. Will they go to Amazon, Craigslist, eBay? Why or why not?
- Based on this, do you need an ecommerce website of your own to sell whatever it is?
- Do you need a storefront?
- Do you need a way to distribute your product to certain types of stores?

It boils down to this: How can you make it as easy as possible for people to buy your product? You need to strive to eliminate every possible roadblock.

Promotion

- Concerning promotion, where and when is the best and most economical place to communicate your story and selling message to the target market?
- Will the audience be reached by advertising online, in newspapers or on TV, or radio, or billboards? In what are the specific places or media vehicles?
- When is the best time to promote? When do people make their decisions to buy? Is there seasonality in the market?
- Are there any wider environmental issues that suggest or dictate the timing of your market launch, or the timing of subsequent promotions?
- How do your competitors promote? How should their strategies and tactics influence the promotional activity for your product?

Many have found the most economical and effective way to promote their wares is to develop an email list of present and potential customers. Do you, or will you go to trade shows or events? Can you collect email addresses there? Perhaps you can offer something on your website, perhaps a free download such as an eBook or brochure containing valuable information that requires them to give you their email addresses. Then you can promote what you have to them with a newsletter and special offerings of one kind or another using an email service like Mail Chimp or Constant Contact.

In summary, it's important to conduct a thorough analysis of the product or service, the customers and stakeholders, as well as its competitors, and the market or markets being served. But do not stop there. This magnifying glass on the product and market should produce enough information to determine how best to set your company and brand apart in a way your target audience will find compelling. Then you will have the information you need to mount a successful marketing campaign.

In the next chapter we will cover more information that you may find helpful in growing your net worth and in developing your plan to launch a business of your own.

CHAPTER SIX: A Short Course in Financial Literacy

In 1957 an Englishman named Cyril Northcote Parkinson [1909-1993] published a book called, *Parkinson's Law,* that explained why government and big business bureaucracies tend to become bloated and inefficient.

His law can be stated as follows:

> "Work expands so as to fill the time available for its completion."

Someone who has all day to get and send a birthday card, for example, will typically take pretty much all day. In the morning, they might go to a store and shop for just the right card. If they don't find it in the first store, they will go to a second, and perhaps a third. Once they find what they are looking for, they will likely come home, have lunch, and spend some serious time thinking of just the right thing to add to the birthday wishes printed on the card. After they come up with something appropriate, write that on the card, sign it, insert it in the envelope, and seal it, they will likely meander out to their car and drive to the post office to stand in line, buy a stamp and mail the card. It could be dinnertime before they arrived back home.

On the other hand, a person who has a list of things to get done, and limited time, might go online, find a website that offers eCards, select one and fire it off to the birthday boy or girl in less than five minutes. This without doubt is why more than 200 years ago Ben Franklin came up with the saying, "If you want a job done, give it to a busy person."

A derivative of Parkinson's Law in the field of finance is something everyone who wants to become wealthy needs to know, understand, and resist:

"Expenses rise to meet income."

You may be thinking, "Really? How is that possible?"

What follows is an example of how it can happen to a middle-class working couple, but be aware the same phenomenon can and will happen in a business if the person in charge doesn't constantly guard against it. So, guard against it.

With that said, let's take a look at a couple I will call William and Hannah—two well-educated individuals, both with good jobs, who decide to get married. Hannah gives up her apartment and moves into William's place in-town. They quickly find they are saving money because "two can live (almost) as cheaply as one." But the apartment is somewhat cramped, and so they decide to put that extra money aside so they can buy a house in the suburbs, have children, and live the American dream. After all, our society suggests that is the right and normal thing to do.

Before long, William and Hannah have saved enough for a down payment, and they buy their dream house in the burbs. Now they have a mortgage and property taxes to pay, sizable utility bills, and of course, the house is a lot bigger than their little apartment was in town. So they buy furniture using credit cards.

Now, in addition to a mortgage, they have credit card debt.

Their first child comes along, and they decide that William's Jeep Wrangler is no longer practical or sufficient, so they trade it in on a used Infiniti sedan for William and a brand new, shiny SUV for Hannah. After all, anything less would look out of place among the McMansions in their swanky neighborhood.

Now they have a mortgage, rising property taxes, big utility bills, credit card debt with an APR of 18 percent, two cars, two car payments, house and auto repair bills, and personal property taxes on both vehicles. But, why worry? William and Hannah are both climbing the corporate ladders where they work, and bringing in much bigger paychecks than when they lived in that little apartment in town.

You see where this is going, so I won't belabor it. William and Hannah make quite a lot of money, but they also spend quite a lot of money, and with each rise in pay they increase their spending. Their expenses keep on rising to gobble up their income just as Parkinson's law predicts, so much so that in some months they actually struggle to get by. If one of them loses his or her job, they will be in serious trouble, which is why in Chapter One I urged you to live below your means and pay yourself first. If you truly want to become wealthy, it's not how much money you make that's important, it's how much money you keep. And you need to put the money you keep to work so that it grows and eventually will pay you dividends.

Let's look at how you might do that.

New Definitions for Assets & Liabilities

In his book *Rich Dad Poor Dad,* Robert T. Kiyosaki wrote that if you want to become rich, Rule Number One is to know the difference between an asset and a liability. The thing is, Kiyosaki's definitions for an asset and a liability are not the same as those you would hear from a CPA. According to an accountant, William and Hannah's house is an asset—probably the biggest asset they will ever own, particularly since they spend every penny they make and do not have any money left over to buy much else of value. But by Kiyosaki's definition, William and Hannah's house is a liability—not an asset—because it costs them money in the form of a mortgage, upkeep, utility bills, and real estate taxes. For Kiyosaki, an asset isn't an asset unless it is paying you. For him to call it an "asset," it has to be putting money in your pocket.

His advice, and my advice, is to use the money you pay yourself each month to buy what truly are assets—investments that put your money to work making more money for you. Kiyosaki would say that's what rich people do. Middle class people, on the other hand, buy what accountants may call assets, but what in reality are liabilities—such as the houses they live in and the fancy cars and SUVs they use to chauffer their kids to and from soccer matches.

As has been said, the poor and middle class work for money. The rich let money work for them. Think about it. If, for example, William and Hannah had not purchased a big house in the suburbs, but rather had remained a few more years in their apartment and invested the money they were able to save in rental property or stock funds, they would probably now own several rental houses that are paying for themselves. If they had put the money in stocks, they would be getting dividends from stocks. Either way, they would be building equity while generating excess cash each month. It can be argued that thinking that a house you buy to live in is an investment, along with the philosophy that a pay raise means you can buy a bigger house or a fancier car, is the cause of today's debt-ridden, financially shaky society.

To sum up, allowing expenses to rise unchecked to meet income can put a family into greater debt and increased financial uncertainty, even though mom and dad may be advancing in their careers and getting regular pay raises. Instead, it makes a lot more sense to keep liabilities and expenses down so that more money can be put into true assets—assets that that generate money that can be reinvested.

Questionable Net Worth Versus True Wealth

Let's say William and Hannah's McMansion in the suburbs is now worth a million dollars, a number of years have passed, and they have paid the mortgage down to $500,000. And let's say the shiny SUV they bought for $70,000 together with the Infiniti is now worth $50,000 and they only have $25,000 left to pay. And of course, there's also the furniture in their house and some golf clubs William bought for which he paid a bundle. Let's say an estate sale and liquidation would bring in $10,000. That means William and Hannah have a net worth of $535,000 ($1,000,000 - $500,000 + 50,000 - $25,000 + $10,000 = $535,000).

But what if a recession hits and William or Hannah, or perhaps even both of them lose their jobs? How long would they survive?

Not long.

Would they have to sell their house?

Yes, probably, but in a recession they might have trouble finding a buyer, especially for a million dollar house.

So you might say the fact they have a $535,000 net worth on paper is really not worth much more than the paper it's printed on. If William and Hannah are unable to sell their house to get cash out to live on, and if they cannot pay the mortgage because one or both are out of work, the mortgage company will foreclose on their house. If and when that happens, they will lose the house and be out on the street—pretty much penniless.

It seems to me a better way to measure wealth is the one Robert Kiyosaki suggested in his book mentioned above.

"Wealth," he writes, "is a person's ability to survive so many number of days forward—or, if I stopped working today, how long could I survive?"

He goes on to say that so-called net worth as calculated according to accountants often includes non-cash-producing assets such as, "stuff you bought that now sits in your garage." Wealth, according to his definition, is how much money your money is making for you, and therefore, your financial survivability. By this measurement, if you have expenses of $5,000 per month and receive income from cash-producing assets of $5,000 per month, you could survive indefinitely, and by Kiyosaki's definition, that would make you wealthy indeed.

How to Keep Your Day Job and Still Get Rich

Robert Kiyosaki kept his day job until he retired at age 47. But it wasn't money from his job that enabled him to retire. He became rich by investing in real estate. Kiyosaki started with houses, never keeping any one property more than seven years. He continued trading up, using U.S. tax laws to his advantage to avoid paying capital gains, until he eventually owned a number of apartment and office buildings that paid him enough to be able to spend each day in his own way.

The capital gains tax for most Americans is 15 percent. So if you buy a rental property for $100,000, and turn around and sell it for $200,000, you would have a capital gain of $100,000 and owe the government $15,000—unless you know how to avoid paying it. I should note parenthetically, however, that those earning adjusted incomes of more than $464,850 will pay a 20 percent Federal tax on their capital gains above that amount, according to current (2018) law.

That's still a lot less than the top Federal tax on earned income, which as of tax year 2018 is 35 percent on incomes between $200,000 and $500,000 for married couples filing separately, and 39.6 percent on incomes over $500,000. This is one reason big corporations use stock options to reward their top executives. For example, a Senior Vice President might be given an option to buy 10,000 company shares at $20 per share. If the stock goes to $50 per share, when he buys the stock and then sells it, he will make $300,000 (10,000 x $50 = $500,000 minus 10,000 x $20 = $200,000, for a gain of $300,000).

Not only does this give the executive an incentive to do his or her best to increase the value of the company's stock—which is what the shareholders of the company want—when the executive cashes in, he or she will pay a capital gains tax of $45,000, rather than the much higher earned-income tax of $105,000, thereby saving $60,000. (15% x 300,000 = $45,000 versus 35% x $300,000 = $105,000; $105,000 minus $45,000 = $60,000.)

So, how did Robert Kiyosaki avoid paying capital gains taxes? He took advantage of a rule to be found under section 1031 of the United States IRS Code known as "a 1031 Exchange." To put it simply, this allows an investor to defer paying capital gains taxes on an investment property when it is sold, as long another "like-kind property" is purchased with the profit gained by the sale of the first property. This made it possible for Kiyosaki to build a much larger real estate empire than would have been possible otherwise. In his book, he gives an example of how he made more than half a million dollars from an initial investment made in 1989 of $5,000.

He lived in Portland, Oregon at the time, the timber market was depressed, and there were "For Sale" signs everywhere on houses. As he was jogging in a neighborhood one day, he noticed a For Sale sign that looked like it had been up for a while in front of a cute little house that appeared to be rather old. He saw the owner in the yard and stopped and asked him what he was asking for the house.

"Make me an offer," the owner said.

Apparently the house had been for sale from more than a year and no one was interested. Kiyosaki put $5,000 down and bought the house for $45,000, which was $20,000 less than the asking price. He then rented the house, and after paying the mortgage, upkeep and other expenses with the rent money, he cleared $40 a month. Not a big deal, you will agree.

A year later, however, the housing market in Portland began to pick up. Californians used to paying a lot more for housing were moving up the coast to Oregon, and Kiyosaki sold the little house to one of them for $95,000. The capital gain of about $40,000 plus his original down payment of $5,000, for a total of $45,000 was put in a 1031 tax-deferred exchange, and he went shopping. About a month later, he made a low-ball offer on a 12-unit apartment building. The asking price was $450,000, and he was able to get it for $300,000.

Kiyosaki held that building for two years and then sold it for $495,000. By that time, he and his wife had moved to Phoenix, Arizona. Apparently the real estate market in Phoenix happened to be depressed at that time. Using a 1031 tax- deferred exchange, he used the gain and the equity from the sale of the apartment building in Portland to invest in a 30-unit apartment building in Phoenix that he was able to buy for $875,000. Cash flow from the units was more than $5,000 per month.

Eventually, the real estate market in Phoenix rebounded, and Kiyosaki sold that apartment building for $1.2 million.

A Guide to Prosperity

So, with an initial investment of $5,000, he made a profit of $565,000.

Here's a quick review: With $5,000 down, he bought a house for $45,000 that he sold for 95,000 for a gain of $50,000. For $50,000 down, he bought an apartment building for $300,000 that he sold for $495,000 for a gain of $195,000 + $50,000 = $245,000.

For $245,000 down, he bought an apartment building for $875,000 that he later sold for $1.2 million for a gain of $570,000. ($1,200,000 minus $875,000 = $325,000 + $245,000 equity = $570,000.)

It should go without saying that Robert Kiyosaki had some lucky breaks and definitely benefited from good timing. A lot of people trying to do something similar back when the real estate bubble burst in the Great Recession of 2008-10 were not so lucky and lost their shirts. But people with money, resources, and foresight were able to pick up some very good bargains during the Great Recession and now are reaping the benefits. The real estate gods giveth and they taketh away.

The point of this case history is that it is possible to become wealthy and still keep your day job if you are willing to live below your means and take some risks. Keep expenses low, reduce liabilities, and diligently build a base of solid assets that generate income. Just imagine where William and Hannah might be today if they had followed that path. As their cash flow grew, and they reached a point where they no longer needed day jobs to survive, they could have begun to indulge in some luxuries. That's what delayed gratification is all about.

A Guide to Prosperity

The time is near for me to bring this book to a close, but let me say that an important point I hope I have made is that rich people buy luxuries last, while the poor and the middle class tend to buy them first. Why bother working for money and then spend it all in order to keep up with the Jones? Wouldn't it be better to let money work for you so that you will reach a point in life—under the age of 50 if at all possible—when you are able to spend each day in your own way?

Here are a few thoughts I'd like to leave with you, some of which I have touched upon already, but that I believe bear reinforcement. Do these things, and you are bound to enjoy a successful life:

- Always under promise and over deliver.
- Seek harmony in all that you do.
- Put aside an emergency fund.
- Develop a top credit rating so that you will always be able to borrow money.
- Hire great people.
  Put other people's money and talents to work to grow your business.
- Be authentic. Talk the talk and walk the walk.
- Be a person of great character and integrity.
- Lead by example and build a championship team.
- Don't waste money, be frugal, and value every dollar you spend.
- Save at least ten to fifteen percent of your income every month and invest it in real estate or in stock funds that charge a low fee and that mirror a diversified market portfolio.

- Graduate high school, go to college, and earn a marketable degree.
- Read, read, and read some more. Continue learning and developing yourself throughout your entire life.
- Build a personal and professional network. You get rich through and with others.
- Be involved in the world. Volunteer, travel, and discover your passion.
- Become an expert in your field.
- Own revenue producing, positive-cash-flow real estate, and dividend-paying stocks.
- Start a business, grow a business, and sell a business.

I have written this book because I know how much it would have helped me to have read it when I was young, just starting out. It would also have been a huge help if I had read it before I started a business. Unfortunately, very little of what I have just shared with you is taught in school or college. Almost all of them are in the business of preparing their students for jobs, not to start their own businesses. As a result, it has taken me more than 40 years—all the way past retirement age—to learn much of it through a number of mistakes I made along the way. Believe me when I say, some of those mistakes were very painful and difficult to overcome.

I'm reminded of a sign that was in the creative department bullpen of the ad agency where I worked right out of college. It said in big bold letters:

LEARN FROM THE MISTAKES OF OTHERS.
YOU DON'T HAVE TIME TO MAKE
THEM ALL YOURSELF.

That's great advice that I hope you will follow.

Let me close by saying, I sincerely hope this book will help you on your path to wealth, success, and the ability to spend each day in your own way.

Take it and run with it.

This Book Summarized in Brief

I've included this chapter by chapter summary of the key points I hope to have made with the thought that you may wish to use it periodically to refresh your memory and to recharge your entrepreneurial batteries.

CHAPTER ONE: Your Road to Riches

A premise of this book is that all those who are capable of earning a living—of getting and holding a job—can become wealthy if they start with enough time ahead of them and systematically take certain actions.

Most people are not rich because they have a job. The rich don't trade their labor, time, and talent for money. They let money work for them.

There are very few jobs that pay enough to make a person rich. Being highly skilled is important and something to strive for, but to become wealthy—really wealthy—you need to get on something besides the job ladder. You need to switch to the passive income ladder—the one the richest people are on. On this ladder you acquire money, and ultimately wealth, without exchanging your time, talent, and labor for it. You do this by acquiring assets that produce money for you—even while you're sleeping.

You should pick a company to work for not because it pays the best, but because it is the one that will give you the best opportunity to learn a business and hone your craft. There, you will be exchanging your time and labor for money while you get really good at what you do and at the same time study and learn everything there is to know about the business and the market it serves. In the meantime, you ought to put aside at least ten percent of your income so that it produces passive income that's continually reinvested.

Step One on the Road to Riches

If you are willing to take risks, your goal ought be to become so good at what you do that eventually you will be able to quit your job and do what you do for customers or clients that will pay you directly for your work without an employer in the middle taking a cut. That is Step One on your road to riches. After taking Step One, your next goal will be to grow your business to a point you cannot handle it all yourself. Then you will hire someone and pay him or her a salary to help you service your customers. When that happens you will have become an employer and you will begin to reap profits from work done by others. An example given in this chapter is that plumbers make about $25 per hour, but plumbing companies charge on average about $122.50 per hour for their work. Even after adding the cost of a support staff and overhead such as rent and equipment, a plumbing company should be making a good profit on each and every plumber it can keep busy.

CHAPTER TWO: Chart Your Course

If you are in a job you hate, it's time to change. If you are just starting out, do not seek out the highest paying job you can qualify for and find. If you love teaching, for example, do not become an accountant just because it pays more. Do what you love, but realize that as long as you are working for someone else, it will be unlikely that you will get rich.

Set aside a full day. Go to a library or some other secluded place. Take a pen a legal pad, find a quiet spot, and get comfortable. You are there to decide what to do with the rest of your life. Nothing could be more important. Ask yourself this question:

What have I done that puts me totally in the zone so that when I finish, I look up and see that hours that have passed and it seemed like only minutes?

Once you have identified what that is, you need to figure out how to use that activity in service to others. It's your "in-the-zone" activity and it's what can make you rich. Identify your gift and develop a plan to get off the job track and onto the path to creating a business that puts it to work.

There are basically four types of businesses:

1. High-Energy, Low-Margin

A High-Energy, Low-Margin business is one that is complicated, tricky, employee intensive, capital intensive, inventory intensive, very competitive, and to make things really bad, it doesn't make much money. An example is grocery store in a competitive market.

2. High-Energy, High-Margin

The High-Energy, High-Margin category includes businesses such real estate development and construction; the building trades—plumbing, electrical, mechanical, HVAC, etc.—road building. Such businesses tend to be employee intensive, capital intensive, complicated and tricky, but they can make a lot of money. The more employees you can keep busy, the more money you can make because you can make a profit on each.

3. Low-Energy, High-Margin

The Low-Energy, High-Margin category is the best one to be in if you can pull it off. Creativity and brainpower drive these businesses, and they are easily scalable. Typically, tech companies, software companies, and some import-export companies fit into this category. Apple Computer is a prime example. High tech tools of all kinds that are developed and designed in the U.S., manufactured in low-wage countries around the world such as China and Vietnam, and sold through retailers across the USA can be gold mines. So are companies that rely on specialty software such as Uber, Google, Facebook, Lyft, and Airbnb.

4. Low-Energy, Low-Margin

A Low-Energy, Low-Margin business is one that's fun and easy, but doesn't make much money.

As you develop your plan, look for the obstacles in your way. Once you identify them, the hard work is done because now all you need to do is figure out ways to get around them, over them, or under them. The course you devise to skirt the obstacles will be your action plan—the path to take you where you want to go.

An alternative to starting a business is to buy an existing one in your field, possibly out of the profits and without much money down. All businesses are for sale. Often a business owner feels trapped. He'd like to unload the business but doesn't want to put it on the market because his employees would find out and might start looking elsewhere for jobs. If a particular business interests you, it may make sense talk to the owner and find out.

CHAPTER THREE: Starting and Growing a Business

Ralph was an average kid who went into the business school of his university to avoid having to take science courses. Money and finance, it turned out, was his in-the-zone field. After graduation, he took a job at a bank and became a loan officer where he learned the ins and outs of building construction finance. Ralph decided to go into the construction business, but his lack of knowledge of and of contacts was the obstacle standing in his way.

Ralph recalled that a high school acquaintance, George, worked for a big construction firm. Ralph put together a plan that laid out all the numbers for George, and the two of them agreed to go into business. Over the course of 25 years, they built a real estate development and construction firm with offices in two states that built hundreds of houses a year. They sold that firm for more than $200 million.

Ralph benefited from leveraging money. By understanding what was important to banks, he as able to develop construction-financing proposals that bank loan officers would approve. In that way he was able to put other people's money to work to build his business.

Jason is a guy who knew one thing for sure: He wanted to work for himself. He learned the vending machine business from a part-time job he had in college and bought a vending route after graduation with a small down payment. He kept adding vending routes and growing that business, and then used some of the proceeds to by an answering service business. He put it together with another answering service business and expanded into other telecom services. He then sold that business and used the money to buy other businesses. While he is now very wealthy, he almost lost it all during a recession because he allowed himself to become over-leveraged and he also had two High-Energy, Low-Margin businesses that were losing money because of the downturn. The lesson he learned was not to go so far out on a limb, borrowing so much money, and to only invest in or start Low-Energy, High-Margin businesses if at all possible.

Selling a Business

There are plenty of companies that will help you sell your business, and so before you select one, you would be wise to talk to a number, let them give you a pitch, and contact their references.

There are basically three kinds: business brokers, M&A advisors and investment bankers.

Business brokers typically work with smaller companies, businesses that will likely be purchased by an individual buyer, rather than a corporation. Restaurants, retail shops, convenience stores, and gas stations are examples that fall into this category. The process business brokers use is very similar to that of listing a house for sale with a real estate agent, and the terms are similar. Typically, they handle sales that are $2 million or less. Investment bankers handle those above $250 million, and M&A advisors work in the gap between the two.

M&A advisors and investment bankers typically sell companies to and for other companies or institutional investors such as private equity funds. Both M&A advisors and investment bankers will play one potential buyer against another with the goal of maximizing the dollar value of the sale. They will put together a thick book about a business—one that's full of details about every aspect of the company—and send it out to all the potential strategic and institutional buyers. Often they will do so with a deadline to receive sealed bids and offers.

The Story of Dave and Marie

The genesis of Dave and Marie's business was the Iraq War. Dave worked for a high-tech firm that had government contracts. The U.S. Army had purchased a software system Dave had helped develop, and he was sent to Iraq to provide training and support. Dave saw firsthand how desperate people in a populated area can become when the electric grid is no longer reliable, and basic services, such as sanitation and trash removal, were no longer in operation.

A few years after he returned from Iraq, Dave met and married Marie, a marketing executive for a large company. They both liked the peace and quiet of the countryside, and moved some distance from the city where they both worked to a home that got its water from a well. During a power outage caused by an ice storm, Dave was reminded of his time in Bagdad because, without electricity, a twenty-first century well doesn't work. Dave's realized a gasoline generator would not be a good solution during an extended period without power, so he rigged up a system that used a solar panel and battery backup to run the well pump.

Dave lost his job during the Great Recession of 2008-2010, and Marie encouraged him to see if he could find a way to use that solar panel system as an initial building block for a company. Dave put an ad on Craigslist for a solar panel system that would power a well pump, and he got a surprisingly large response. Dave soon took another step forward and began installing solar panel systems with back-up battery banks that could run an entire house off grid.

Marie quit her job and went to work with Dave and put her marketing skills to work for the new firm. Today Dave and Marie have the largest company in their region of the country that's in the business of installing residential solar power systems with backup energy storage.

Startup Business Possibilities

Let's say you have identified what puts you in the zone and have developed a business plan, but you don't want to take a chance and quit your job. It may make sense to test the waters to find out if there is a market, and thereby ease into a transition. You might try selling a product or service on Craigslist, for example, or one of the many venues on the Internet that now exist for people looking for gigs, or to sell their wares. Then deliver the product or service during evenings or weekends or on days you don't have to work at your regular job.

CHAPTER FOUR: Develop the Right Attitude

Having the right attitude is critical for success because you unconsciously take actions based on your thoughts and attitudes. If you think of yourself as a victim of circumstances, for example, you will most certainly be a victim of circumstances. If you think of yourself as rich—that you deserve to be rich because it is your birthright—with a sufficient amount of effort, you will become rich. That is the message of two of the most popular self-help and get-rich books of all time: *Think, and Grow Rich* by Napoleon Hill [1883-1970] and *The Science of Getting Rich* by Wallace D. Wattles [1860-1911].

You may think that you cannot help what thoughts enter your mind, and that may be true. But you can decide which thoughts to keep and which thoughts to throw away. Ultimately, what's in your mind is your destiny. Over time, the outer conditions of your life will come to be in tune with your inner state. James Allen [1864-1912] wrote a terrific little book about this called, *As a Man Thinketh*.

Your subconscious mind is under the control of your conscious (objective) mind. As a result, it will work to bring into reality whatever your conscious mind believes and feels is true. Moreover, the subconscious mind does not understand or hear the words "no" and "not." Therefore, you should always phrase self-talk in a positive way—as in, "Make this serve an ace!" rather than, "Don't double fault!"

Think positive and rid yourself of fears

Fears create subconscious programming that can lead to failure and can be grouped under one of six headings:

- the fear of poverty (or failure),
- the fear of criticism,
- the fear of ill health,
- the fear of the loss of love,
- the fear of old age,
- and the fear of death.

How do you get rid of them? Shoo them away. As President Roosevelt once said, "There is nothing to fear but fear itself."

The Power of Positive Thinking

There is power in positive thinking. The problem is, many of us today were not taught that as children, and in fact, feelings of frustration, discontent, and dissatisfaction were ways of solving problems that many of us "learned" as infants. If a baby is hungry, he or she expresses discontent by crying, and a tender hand appears magically and brings a bottle of milk. This "works" for infants, and for some children. But it does not work in adult life when a person is out in the world on his or her own. Which employee do you suppose is most likely to get promoted, the one who constantly complains? Or the one with a positive attitude that consistently delivers the goods?

A positive attitude is vitally important to success, but it is not all that is needed. "Belief" is the most important factor. You can be as positive as Santa Claus, but if you still worry and have doubts in spite of your positive thoughts, you're throwing monkey wrenches into the workings of your subconscious mind.

Be likeable and Appealing to Others

Becoming rich will require effort and work, and that means things will be easier if you have help along the way. The most likely source of that help will be friends, partners, and mentors. Obviously, the going will be easier and you will attract more help if people like you and want to work with you. Therefore, it's important to be someone others want to be around—someone people like and want as a friend. That means you need to be someone who "talks the talk," and "walks the walk."

This is not to say you shouldn't be competitive. It's important to have a winning attitude. Winning surely beats the alternative, and people want to go with a winner—they want to "hitch their wagon to a star." But it's also important to understand that you should never gloat about winning—never rub in it—and realize that sometimes as big a payoff will come in the form of goodwill if are a gracious loser.

Obey the Laws of Physics

Newton's Third Law of Motion states that "For every action, there is an equal and opposite reaction." Throw a rock into a pond, and you will disturb the harmony of the pond. You were the cause, and the effect was the splash. The ripples flow out, and they flow back until harmony is restored. In the same way, disharmonious actions by a person go out into the world and come back upon back upon that person until harmony is restored. That is why it is always best to "live and let live," and to follow the Golden Rule, which is to "Do unto others as you would have others do unto you." Do this and the good you do will return to you. It is also the reason you should always under promise and over deliver. Do that and you will enjoy repeat business time after time.

Develop Healthy Self Esteem

As you contemplate your future course, it is also important to realize you can only attract that which you feel worthy of. Self-esteem is critical to success. Fear and negative programming are all that can prevent you from realizing your full potential. The more you can let go of the fears, the higher your self esteem will be, and the more options you will have and the more risks you can take.

You can have anything you want if you can give up the belief you cannot have it and replace it with the belief you can. Of course, you must get the education necessary and learn the skills you need to create what you want.

Finally, when considering your new challenge, your path to riches, you may want to consider whether it is something you will do alone, or if it can be more readily accomplished in cooperation with others. When two or more people of similar purpose come together to accomplish that purpose, their combined energy directed toward the attainment of it is doubled, tripled, quadrupled, or more.

Be a Strong Leader and Develop a Great Team

The success of a business enterprise typically comes as a result of the skills, attitudes, and actions of everyone down the line pulling together to move forward and this requires strong leadership. While much has been written about leadership, it seems to me that leadership can be boiled down to a single core attribute—a leader's personal commitment to the company, the team, or the objective everyone has bought into. That commitment is what encourages people to follow. Personal commitment compels an individual to take the necessary actions and to have the courage to follow through and persevere until the goal is reached.

Personal commitment aligns the thoughts and minds of the leader and the team so that the sum is greater than the parts and even unconscious actions lead toward positive results.

Take Time to Make a Life

Perhaps you have heard the saying, "Never become so busy making a living that you do not have time to make a life." That's advice worth taking that should start with doing what's necessary to maintain a healthy balance between your work life and your home life.

CHAPTER FIVE: Be Conscious of and Build Your Brand

David N. Martin [1930-2012] co-founder of The Martin Agency, defined a brand as, "a name that stands for something—one that conveys an expectation of performance." If you accept Martin's definition, some people's names are brands.

What do you want people to think when they hear your name?

If you answered, "A mover and shaker—the go-to person in his or her field—who is genuinely a good guy or gal and fun to work with," then follow the advice given in Chapter Four. That's what will make you someone people want to work with and be around. A good reputation is worth more than money can buy so make sure that is what you develop and maintain through the actions you take and the ways in which you conduct yourself and relate to others. It pays to guard your reputation. Choose the right friends and associates. Be of great character, keep your word and do the right things. Follow that advice and you cannot go wrong.

It's vitally important that you and your product or company be authentic—the real deal. Something marketing executives agree on is that, "Nothing kills a bad product (brand) faster than good advertising." That means you and your business must deliver on the promise and the image projected by your communications, or people will drop you and your product like a hot potato.

Are you on LinkedIn, Facebook, Instagram, and so forth? What do your social media sites say about you? If they don't reflect the real you and the image you want to project, they need to be changed so that they do.

A Guide to Prosperity

Do you have a website? If not, you need one, and what people see there and learn from it needs to reflect the authentic you. Everything people will see online when they Google your name needs work together to tell your story because more than anything, your story is what will create your brand image.

You may think people will choose you and your product if you give them enough good reasons to do so—such as lots of good features and benefits and a completive price—but that's only partly true. We human beings aren't as rational as we like to think we are. No one makes totally rational decisions. This means that facts about your brand are important to your audience, but only secondarily. People make purchase decisions—and all kinds of decisions—on the basis of emotion, then look for facts and rational arguments to justify their emotional decisions. That's why it's important to have a story to tell in order to build a bond with potential customers.

Almost all compelling stories boil down to the same essential plot: A sympathetic character—the hero—ventures from his or her everyday world into a place or region unlike any he or she has known before. Forces are encountered that attempt to destroy the hero, but the hero perseveres and pushes forward in what may seem like a lost cause. Even so, after a great struggle, and a dark moment when all seems lost, a victory is won. The hero then returns home in possession of the elixir and lives happily ever after.

We relate to this story because our lives are one hero's journey after another. We typically face a series of trials and tribulations—Hero's Journeys—as the years role by. Most of them work out, and we return home with the elixir—wiser and more evolved than when we left. That's why we root for and identify with others who have faced and overcome difficulties.

What's Your Story? What drives or motivates you? Why did you decide to start the company? What happened to create that drive or cause that decision? For Dave, it was what he saw in Iraq.

The Four Ps of Marketing

The discipline of marketing is based on "The Four Ps." Thinking about them in light of the company you're planning to create can help you develop a brand and marketing strategy. Let's take a look:

> Product (or Service)
> Place (where sold or how distributed)
> Price
> Promotion

It's important to conduct a thorough analysis of the product or service, the customers and stakeholders, as well as its competitors, and the market or markets being served. But do not stop there. This magnifying glass on the product and market should produce enough information for you to determine how best to set your company and brand apart in a compelling way in order to mount a successful marketing campaign.

CHAPTER SIX: A Short Course in Financial Literacy

A derivative of Parkinson's Law is that, "Expenses rise to meet income."

William and Hannah allowed themselves to get into a difficult situation because of this. When they first were married, they were in position to save a lot of money and invest it in income producing assets, but instead they decided to follow conventional wisdom and societal norms. They bought a McMansion in the suburbs and now they have a mortgage, rising property taxes, big utility bills, credit card debt with an APR of 18 percent, two cars, two car payments, house and auto repair bills, and personal property taxes on both vehicles. In some months they struggle to get by. If one of them loses his or her job, they will be in serious trouble.

A New Definition of Assets & Liabilities

Robert T. Kiyosaki wrote that if you want to become rich, Rule Number One is to know the difference between an asset and a liability, but his definitions for "asset" and "liability" are not the same as those from a CPA. For Kiyosaki, an asset isn't an asset unless it is paying you. For him to call it an "asset," it has to be putting money in your pocket. As has been said, the poor and middle class work for money. The rich let money work for them. If William and Hannah had not purchased a big house in the suburbs, but instead had invested the money in rental property while living in William's in-town apartment, they would probably now own several rental houses and have assets generating cash for them each month.

Questionable Net Worth Versus True Wealth

We calculated that by conventional accounting practices, William and Hannah have a net worth of $535,000. Even so, if one or both lose their job, they would not be able to survive very long. If they are unable to sell their house to get cash out to live on, and if they could not pay the mortgage, the bank will foreclose, and they will lose everything.

Therefore, a better way to measure wealth is to calculate how long a person would survive if he or she stopped working. By this measure, if someone has expenses of $5,000 per month and receives income from cash-producing assets of $5,000 per month, that individual would be able to survive indefinitely, which would make him or her a wealthy person.

We also learned that it is possible to keep a day job and still get rich. Robert Kiyosaki did so by investing in real estate. He continued trading up, using U.S. tax laws to his advantage to avoid paying capital gains, until he eventually owned a number of apartment and office buildings that paid him enough to be able to spend each day in his own way.

How did he avoid paying capital gains taxes? He took advantage of a rule under section 1031 of the United States IRS Code known as "a 1031 Exchange," which allows an investor to defer paying capital gains taxes on an investment property when it is sold, as long another "like-kind property" is purchased with the profit gained by the sale of the first property. This made it possible for Kiyosaki to build a much larger real estate empire than otherwise would have been possible.

In his book, *Rich Dad Poor Dad,* Kiyosaki gives an example of how he made more than half a million dollars from an initial investment of only $5,000. He had some lucky breaks and definitely benefited from good timing, but the point is that it can be done.

Imagine where William and Hannah might be today if they had followed that path.

An important point of this book is that rich people buy luxuries last, while the poor and the middle class tend to buy them first. Wouldn't it be better to let money work for you so that you will reach a point in life when you are able to spend each day in your own way? You can do so simply by adhering to a few basic principles.

www.ingramcontent.com/pod-product-compliance
Lightning Source LLC
Chambersburg PA
CBHW072210170526
45158CB00002BA/539